KATAHDIN *Woods & Waters* NATIONAL MONUMENT

KATAHDIN *Woods & Waters* NATIONAL MONUMENT

ERIC E. HENDRICKSON

Published by The History Press
Charleston, SC
www.historypress.com

Front cover image is looking south out over the monument from the top of Deasey Mountain. Back cover image is looking upstream at the first drop of Haskell Rock Pitch.

First published 2020

Manufactured in the United States

ISBN 9781467144179

Library of Congress Control Number: 2020934326

CONTENTS

ACKNOWLEDGEMENTS

The goal of this book is to give information on the general history of logging in this area, as well the geology that shaped the land to make it what it is today. It is not, nor was it meant to be, a guide to locations within the monument to find artifacts. Although the author has exhaustively researched many sources for accuracy and completeness of the information, there may be errors because, at times, it is difficult to separate fact from folklore. In many cases, information has been labeled as folklore within the text. In the collection of materials for this book, I have to acknowledge those individuals who recorded their adventures into the wilderness in years past: George Hallowell, the Boston artist who followed and photographed the men working in the woods, and Myron Avery, the great explorer who collected photos and wrote articles documenting the history of the area. Thank you to Bert Call, Lucius Merrill, L. Rogers, the Appalachian Mountain Club (AMC) and Carl Sprinchorn, who allowed a look at their adventures through stories and photographs. The work done by Robert Newman, Gary Boone and others in the area of geology and the natural history of the area was invaluable. There are many others who have helped to document the value of this area for the future of the people of the United States.

I have to acknowledge the encouragement to write this book by the many people who have read about the history of the monument and their willingness to share their photos and articles. Rhonda Brophy from the Lumbermen's Museum not only helped but also gave encouragement for the project and directed me toward people with a story to tell about the history. Bart DeWolf allowed me to tag along on his adventures. Earl Raymond shared his focus on the early surveyors and what they accomplished. John Neff shared historical materials and opened my eyes to historical research. Mike Williams gave me insight into the Civilian Conservation Corps (CCC) workings through his photos and stories. Roger Getz from University of Maine at Presque Isle helped with the understanding of archive operations at the university libraries. There are others who offered photographs that helped tell the story of the monument: Michelle Benoit, Kathy Durr, Roger Merchant, Trudy Wyman of the Millinocket Historical Society, James Nyman (regional archaeologist, National Park Service) and Tim Hudson (superintendent, Katahdin Woods and Waters National Monument). I also have to acknowledge the person who tromps through the forest of the monument with me looking for these natural and historical locations: my wife, Elaine Hendrickson.

I have to acknowledge the Patten Lumbermen's Museum, which is located just outside Patten on Route 159. The museum was founded in 1958 in a Patten Store front, and then a log cabin was moved from Mount Chase to the current location in 1963. The current museum was established in 1963

It was the dream of Lore Rogers (*left*) and Caleb Scribner (*right*) to create a museum that would document the life of the area woodsmen. *Patten Lumbermen's Museum.*

by Lore Rogers and Caleb Scribner, who also served as the first curators; it was a nonprofit educational organization whose mission was to record the graphic history of the lumbermen's world as it once existed in the forests of northern Maine. The museum preserves Maine's logging history and educates the public about the logging heritage and accomplishments of Maine's early inhabitants. Over the years, the museum has developed a number of logging exhibits to help the visitors better understand the life in the wilderness. Exhibits include an 1820 logging camp, a bateau, a Lombard hauler, a working blacksmith shop and woods and lumber camp equipment. In all, the nine buildings have more than five thousand artifacts on display.

The museum has two special events each year to celebrate early logging in the Northwoods. On the third Saturday in May, it has the Fiddlehead Fest. While fiddlers fiddle, cooks compete in the Cast Iron Chef Cook Off, all while artisans, craftsmen and food vendors complete the event. The Annual Bean-Hole Bean Dinner is held on the second Saturday in August. This is the time to see how cooks prepared meals in lumber camps and taste some of the same food eaten by the early lumbermen. Thanks also to Dom and Jarrod at Little Outdoor Giants for their brilliant color photography, which we were able to feature on the cover of the book.

INTRODUCTION

Katahdin Woods and Waters National Monument is an 87,563-acre U.S. National Monument operated by the National Park Service. The monument, located in north-central Maine, Penobscot County, is wild, with picturesque landscapes offering spectacular views of Mount Katahdin. It allows the visitor to discover its pristine rivers and streams, its biodiverse forests with its varied flora and fauna, its logging past and its unique geology. For millennia, it has greeted visitors with night views that are some of the darkest found anywhere on the planet. The monument was formed using a gift from Roxanne Quimby, a cofounder of Burt's Bees. The gift was given to the federal government, which included $40 million to help fund the initial operations of the monument. After the land was donated, President Barack Obama, under the Antiquities Act, designated it by proclamation to become Katahdin Woods and Waters National Monument on August 23, 2016.

While the lands have had a great deal of history and the area has been known by native people since the last glaciation more than eleven thousand years ago, we will look at what shaped the land and the timber era of cultural history. The native peoples depended on this area for both its waterways for travel and the forest for sustenance. Yearly, the people would travel from the coast to the interior and return with meat, fish, native plants for medicines and animal furs. The Penobscot people of the Wabanaki Nation consider the Penobscot River and Katahdin as a centerpiece of their culture.

While the native people used the land, little is known about their travels outside of cultural stories. Therefore, the Katahdin Woods and Waters National Monument gives an opportunity for scientific investigation into the archaeological history of the Native American presence in this area since the most recent period of glaciation.

The first documented Euro-American exploration of the Katahdin region dates back to when, in 1793, Jonathan Maynard and Park Holland were commissioned by the Commonwealth of Massachusetts to do a survey of the area. When Maine became a state in 1820, Joseph Treat and the Penobscot guide John Neptune produced the first detailed map of the area. This was followed by the Monument Line Survey, completed in 1825 by Joseph Norris and his son to establish a township map for the State of Maine. It would be this survey that would open the area to the land barons and what we see today.[1]

While the native people regarded the area as their home, the European immigrants saw it as wilderness. The history of East Branch exploration by nonnative Americans begins with a survey commissioned by the Commonwealth of Massachusetts in 1793. In 1783, shortly after the War of Independence, the commonwealth reached a turning point, facing huge war debts, and its paper currency was worth only 10 percent of its value. It could no longer tax the people, so it turned to sales of its wildlands and opened a land office to survey the lands and place them on the market.[2] In 1793, William Bingham, a land speculator, began acquiring millions of acres in Maine that was to include the contract for an acquisition of 1-million-acre tract in the northern part of the district.[3] Bingham and the Commonwealth of Massachusetts would be unable to close the deal until the land was surveyed.

The 1793 survey of the area was completed by fifty-one-year-old Park Holland of Shrewsbury, Massachusetts, and forty-one-year-old Jonathan Maynard of Framingham, Massachusetts.[4] A few years earlier, they had made their marks as military officers; they were also close friends, which led to their appointment by the State of Massachusetts's Land Committee to survey the lands called the Great East Branch of the Penobscot River.[5] Their task was to survey a tract of land that was six miles wide on both sides of the river to be reserved for the "Indians." They arrived in Bangor on August 8, 1793, to start their work, finally reaching Nicatou[6] at a place they called in their journal the Big Crotch, where the East Branch and West Branch of the Penobscot River join on August 30.[7] On September 1, they decided to break the work up, with

Park Holland pushing east and then north until he reached the French settlements on the St. John River and then heading back to the southwest, finally rejoining Jonathan Maynard somewhere on the East Branch of the Penobscot River. Jonathan Maynard continued up the East Branch, surveying as he went.

Maynard reached the location of the future Hunt Farm on Tuesday, September 3, describing the land in his notes as being wide, flat and fertile. On September 4, he reached the area just below the mouth of the Seboeis River, where he described the land as flat, fertile and growing wild hops as if they were planted in rows. On Wednesday, September 11, he reached Stair Falls and in his field notes described what he calls the handsomest falls he had ever seen in his travels, with eight to ten steps just as in a regular staircase. He finally reached a series of four ponds fifty-three miles upstream, where he saw an otter in the river, so he called the ponds in the river Otter Lake.[8] As the party returned from its push into the wilderness, the men were near starvation; according to folklore, the party had reserved a small dog that had accompanied them as a last resort for a source of food. The little dog saved himself by finding a porcupine, which the party captured and ate. The next day, they came upon an Indian encampment on the banks of the river, where they were given smoked salmon that had been caught and cured by the native peoples. The men feasted until they were nearly all sick from the effects of an overdose of smoked salmon. From his notes, Maynard was able to draw the first very detailed map of this section of Maine. The survey was more than 175 miles longer than expected—far more land had been surveyed than was realized.

Without a doubt, it would be this survey that led the land barons to purchase the lands after Maine became a state. This survey would be the beginning of the push into the wilderness for timber. In their notes, the surveyors described locations that would later become important to the first explorers and lumbermen. The reason for the survey was that at the end of the Revolutionary War, the Treaty of Paris failed to specify a clear highlands boundary between Maine and New Brunswick. The problem was that both countries interpreted the word *highlands* differently. The United States insisted that the "highlands" was the height of land, meaning those lands north of the St. John River watershed; on the other hand, the British felt that the highlands were the height of lands north of the Penobscot River watershed. The area in between these two rivers was a large area rich in wilderness timber, and the survey would help to make clear the boundary by laying claim to the lands that had been surveyed.

The second and more important survey, one that often confuses people visiting the monument, was called the "Monument Line Survey." People become confused when they see the Monument Line on signs and the maps while hiking in Katahdin Woods and Waters National Monument, as they think it has something to do with the NPS designation. The "Monument Line" was a survey line that cuts across the middle of Katahdin Woods and Waters National Monument as well as across Baxter State Park, just to the west of the monument. To understand the "Monument Line," we have to go a bit back in history. At the end of the Revolutionary War, the Treaty of Paris failed to specify a clear boundary between Maine and New Brunswick. In 1796, negotiators ran a "Monument Line" due north from the St. Croix River's headwaters, called Monument Brook, to what was described in the treaty as the "highlands" separating rivers draining into the St. Lawrence from those entering the Atlantic. They agreed on a northern boundary to the newly formed country. If you look at a map of the state of Maine, you can see the straight border on the eastern side of the state above the end of the stream. In 1797, they were able to mark a tree at the headwaters of Monument Brook where the land border would begin. Originally, the marker was a yellow birch tree with a metal barrel hoop around the base. This tree marker was later replaced with a more traditional cedar post marker in 1817[9] and is currently a small metal building with a radio satellite antenna on the top.

But the problem with the description of the border was that both countries still interpreted the word *highlands* differently. The United States insisted that the highlands were the height of lands north of the St. John River that it had surveyed earlier. The British felt that the line should be farther to the south, where the highlands was the height of lands north of the Penobscot River watershed,[10] because the water flowed onto the British lands. The tension would increase as the lumbermen moved into this area to cut timber on the properties. Then, on March 15, 1820, when Maine became an independent state separating from the Commonwealth of Massachusetts, the two states immediately formed the Maine Boundary Commission, which authorized a joint expedition with the British to survey the line.[11] One of the Provisions of the Separation in 1819 was for an equal division of all unsold public lands of Massachusetts within Maine.[12] The lands were to be split evenly between the two states to support the separation. Maine hired Joseph Norris to lay out the boundaries of these unallocated lands in the northern part of Maine so that they could be divided between the two states. The survey would begin with the cedar post boundary marker that had been placed at the headwaters of Monument Brook going from the New Brunswick border straight across the state to the Quebec border to the west. This line would become known as the "Monument Line." Joseph Norris was to mark or blaze the trees along this line and then lay out the townships on a map for the state to use to sell the lands.

While this is an oversimplification of the systems, the townships were six miles square in size and were named using a system of numbers and letters. Townships were designated by "T" for township, with the numbers stating in the east going to the west, and "R" for the range, with the numbers starting in the south going north. The "Monument Line" was the division north to south between T3 and T4 because below that line there were many townships that were already named land grants from before the separation.[13] Some of the towns would eventually be given names, but to this day, many still use the numbering system. The plan also had a provision that one square mile of land in each township would be designated to support the public school in the future when the township was settled and developed.

Joseph C. Norris Sr. and his son ran the line to the west in the summer of 1825. The line they established marks the division between present-day township number 3 and 4 West of the East Line of the State (WELS).[14] By September, they had reached the Seboeis River, at which point they had to leave the woods for other survey work in Washington County. Returning in November, Norris built a raft to cross the Seboeis and continued the line west in the face of a rapidly approaching winter. Crossing the East Branch and then the Wassataquoik, they pushed on to Mount Katahdin, where on November 10, in "intensely cold" winter weather, the party reached an enormous drop-off into the Northwest Basin. The difficulty of the terrain and weather would force them to abandon the survey for the year.[15] The survey was finally completed in 1833. One of the most impressive things about the survey of the line was that it would be another fifty years before another nonnative person would visit the headwaters of the Wassataquoik Valley.

With the Monument Line Survey completed and the townships marked out, the rush to buy land was on in Bangor. With the purchase of whole townships, the lumber barons started to move into the area. But in 1833, things became complicated when the British charged Maine with the "inducement to cut lumber" in the disputed territory. Of course, Maine denied it, but there was worry about a British invasion into the area. In 1839, there was a dispute over timber theft on the disputed lands that culminated in what was called the Aroostook War. Due to the conflict, the roads that accessed the wilderness forests were constructed during this period of border dispute. The Military Road (Route 2) from Bangor to Houlton had been completed; the Aroostook Road (Route 11) from Sherman to Fort Kent had also been completed to support the country's protection of its border and forest wealth. Log forts were also constructed in Fort Kent at the mouth of the Fish River overlooking the St. John River and in Fort Fairfield along the Aroostook River within Maine, while the same thing was happening on the other side of the border in what would become Canada. Meanwhile, the king of the Netherlands had arbitrated a proposal for the border that was accepted by Great Britain but refused by the United States, which was still holding firm to the northern boundary.

As tensions mounted, the federal government finally had to get involved. It came to the point that President Martin Van Buren sent General Winfield Scott to northern Maine with the authority to negotiate a peace or lead the nation into war against Great Britain if things could not be settled without war. Bargaining between General Scott and New Brunswick lieutenant governor John Harvey to avert hostilities calmed things down. The boundary was finally settled in 1842 after negotiations between Daniel Webster and Lord Ashburton of Great Britain culminated in what would become known as the Webster-Ashburton Treaty. In the treaty settlement, the United States received about two-thirds of the disputed lands, which included navigation rights to the St. John River, which is really what it wanted in the first place.[16]

How good were these early surveys compared to today's standards of surveying, and what did they use for tools in making their surveys? There were three primary tools used by the wilderness surveyors. Most of the good surveyors had been trained in the military and were military officers during the wars, using their skills in battle. Each party would have had a calibrated compass that would be used to take the course or bearing that they were following through the forest. The compass would be made of brass, standardized before taken into the field and protected from metal objects and heat, which might affect the readings. Periodically, they would use the stars to verify their location in the forest. They would have had a surveyor's metal chain to mark the distance of each bearing. The chain was introduced in 1620 by Edmond Gunther, who used a one-hundred-link chain that measured 66 feet, with each link being 7.92 inches. While you would think that the surveyor would use a tape of some type, they found that using a chain with a very low coefficient of expansion to be far more rugged and less likely to break or kink. While the length may appear to be random, a measure of ten chains by one chain was 1 acre, and eighty chain lengths was 1 statute mile.[17] The third tool the surveyor used was an instrument called a timber scribe, which was a tool used to mark the corners and lines of a survey. The surveyor would cut down a cedar tree and square it, marking the sides for the boundaries. The cedar beam would then be placed in a pile of rocks as the marker for all the future surveys.[18] These cedar posts are often found in the woods today. All the information was included in a journal the surveyor kept for the landowner. The survey would also include notes on the quality of the soil, the type of forest and anything else that might interest the owner, including the value of the land being traversed by the survey party.

To demonstrate the quality of these early surveys, we will take a look at one of the most famous early wilderness surveys, resurveyed in 1991, called the Epping Survey Baseline 9. This survey played an important part in the establishing of state boundaries and property lines in northern New England and in surveying the eastern United States coast. In 1857, when the United States was emerging as a world nautical power, it was felt that the country needed to be able to measure distances and points more accurately. The need for a baseline was stressed by the United States secretary of war Jefferson Davis. A survey was laid out in 1858 by A.D. Bache, a great-grandson of Benjamin Franklin. The premise of the survey was that if you knew the length of one side and two angles of a triangle, you could calculate the third angle and the length of the other two sides. The triangles were actually a series of triangles within other triangles, using mountaintops as his points of reference. There would be a chain of six major triangles measured, the first being in southwestern Alabama and the last being on the Epping Plain in Washington County, Maine. The length of the other sides of the triangles would be calculated from the known length of the six base lines, which were to be accurately measured.

In the summer of 1857, local farmers had been hired to clear the land and grade it. A.D. Bache had determined that a straight line of just over five miles could be measured. They had to cut into banks or use stone cribbing to elevate the path in order to keep it perfectly level. Four towers were erected to make sure that the line was level. The surveyors used six-foot-long iron bars for their measurements. The bars were encased in a tin tube and supported by trestles. The truly amazing thing about A.D. Bache's measurement was that when it was rechecked in 1991 by a team of professional surveyors using laser-guided Global Positioning Survey (GPS), it was found to be accurate to within one centimeter—less than half an inch. The accuracy of a centimeter over five miles is an amazing feat. When many of the trained army surveyors returning to their regular jobs, they did what they were best at doing: surveying. One could say they did an exceptional job,[19] as this line would become the base for other lines and surveys being done all over the East Coast still today.

You would think, at this point, that the border would finally be settled, but as timber was cut to the north, it had to be sent into New Brunswick to be floated down the St. John River into lands owned by Great Britain. The lumber barons hired a man named Shepard Boody to change the natural flow of the water in the north, returning it to the pre-glacial flow to the south. He constructed two dams, one on Chamberland Lake called Lock Dam and the other on Telos Lake, to raise the water level in Chamberland Lake, where a canal was constructed upstream of the dam that became known as the Telos Cut.

In constructing the Telos Cut, a part of a ridge had to be removed to make the water flow to the south into the Penobscot watershed. This allowed the waters of the upper Allagash River to flow south into the East Branch of the Penobscot instead of north into the St. John River, bringing the timber from the Allagash area downriver to the Bangor market.[20] Today, there are still disputed lands remaining between the two countries. Ten miles off the coast of Maine, you will find the tiny rock island called Machias Seal Island. The island is claimed by both Canada and the United States.

There is a lighthouse on the island maintained by the Canadian Coast Guard but not recognized by the United States government, and a small bird research station is owned by U.S. Fish and Wildlife Service but not recognized by the Canadian government. The island is barren rock, populated by the protected, rare Atlantic puffin, but is visited by researchers, coast guard employees and tour companies from both countries. The tour companies are not allowed to have people from both countries on Machias Seal Island at the same time. If the tours arrive at the same time, one company must wait on the boat until the other company has finished its tour. Recently, in June 2018, the U.S. Border Patrol began stopping fishing vessels, reportedly asking about illegal immigrants. Global Affairs Canada stated that it is investigating, but according to the Canadian Fishermen Association, it was just a routine operation along the disputed border waters.[21]

CHAPTER 1

RECREATIONAL HISTORY

The importance of the monument area can't be looked at without first including some of the early visitors who came to explore the area. The Wassataquoik Stream and Mount Katahdin were considered by many to be the last great wilderness in the East, making it a place for scientists, explorers and artists. The area quickly became an industrial forest in the early years and was incredibly active in the 1800s and early 1900s—men and equipment moved upriver, while the logs floated down the stream, requiring the construction of roads, logging camps and wooden crib dams. The crews used an unimaginable amounts of dynamite to remove the rock left by the glacier both in the streams and where roads and camps were being built. The men would enter the woods in the fall, often with only one set of clothes, cutting timber all winter. Then many of the men would drive the logs downriver to market in the late spring or early summer, just to turn around and do it all over again in the fall. The terrain was extremely difficult, and the winters were harsh, which caused the loggers to develop new and sometime unique methods for cutting timber and moving it to market. The writer Edmund Ware Smith called the Wassataquoik log drives "the most difficult and dramatic of Maine's lumbering history."[22]

Many of those early recreational visitors were from Harvard University in Boston, which at the time was the center of the transcendentalist movement; these visitors generally all knew one another. Transcendentalism was a philosophical movement that developed in 1836 in New England and believed that society—along with its religious as well as political institutions—corrupted the purity of the individual and that only nature in its purest form could bring it back. The transcendentalist believed in three basic values: individualism, idealism and the divinity of nature.[23] We will look at the early visitors' connection to one another and their connection to the logging industry.

The loggers had to establish supply depots along the rivers, which when coupled with better roads from Bangor allowed the first nonnative American explorers and scientists to start coming to the area. In 1793, the Commonwealth of Massachusetts commissioned Jonathan Maynard to survey the East Branch of the Penobscot River. The early understanding of the area was expanded with the 1825 Maine Boundary Commission's authorization of the Monument Line Survey, which marked an important line to be used for a map. Then, in the spring of 1832, the distinguished ornithologist John James Audubon, sketching the flora and fauna for his 1838 publication *Birds of America*, traveled down the Military Road from Houlton to Bangor and remarked about the beauty of the valley below Mount Katahdin. While he never visited the area, I am sure he would have loved to at another time.[24] The first reported person to visit to the Hunt Farm was Charles T. Jackson, first Maine state geologist and a Harvard University graduate, who traveled to the river wilderness in September 1837 carrying out a geological survey for the state to grant it a better understanding of what riches the area held. While Jackson had never visited the region, his sister, Lydia, was married to Ralph Waldo Emerson, who had brought back stories of the area from an earlier Bangor visit.[25] In 1838, Ezekiel Holmes went up the river looking for a water route to Aroostook County using Greenleaf's 1829 map of Maine;[26] as he traveled, he made many comments about the mistakes he found in the maps.

The first recorded ascent of what was probably Mount Katahdin's Hamlin Peak, approaching from the east, was made by Bostonians Edward Everett Hale (grandson of Nathan Hale of Revolutionary War fame) and William Francis Channing (author of *The Man without a Country*), both graduates of Harvard University; in 1845, they wrote about their climb of the mountain. William F. Channing was a scientist, the son of the famous Unitarian theologian William Ellery Channing and a member of Charles Jackson's first survey of New Hampshire. Edward Hale was a Unitarian preacher who was trying to develop, with the help of Ralph Waldo Emerson, a deeper understanding of transcendental philosophy. Both Edward Hale and William Channing were close friends with Henry David Thoreau, who in 1846 followed the original route up Mount Katahdin planned by the Channing/Hale party.[27] That same year, the great mountain guide Reverend Marcus Keep and his friend James H. Haines made their first trip to climb Mount Katahdin, leaving by way of the Hunt Farm, where they blazed a trail as they climbed.

The transcendentalists believed strongly in the equal rights of women and in the antislavery movement. So, Elizabeth Oakes Smith (friends with Henry David Thoreau) and Nancy Crocket Mosman would make the first ascent by a woman of the Katahdin mastiff using the Hunt Farm as a base. Nancy Mosman knew and retained James Haines as their guide because he and Marcus Keep had blazed and cut out a route to Pamola from the Hunt Farm on the East Branch of the Penobscot in 1848. At the same time, Marcus Keep, who had just married Hannah Taylor, planned a trip to climb Mount Katahdin so that his new wife might be the first woman to reach the summit, showing that women were able to do the same things that could be done by men in the wilderness. There are writers who suggest that Elizabeth Smith knew of the Keep trip and wanted to be the first. Smith's trip placed her at the top of Pamola on August 11, 1849, where she left a note on birch bark in a metal top container at the summit for others to find. During their eight-day trip, they covered more than fifty miles and camped just below the summit of Pamola. Smith had written four articles[28] that appeared in the *Portland Daily Advertiser* under the pen name "A Pilgrim," in the true transcendentalist manner. The Smiths' note was discovered by the Keep party when it reached the summit of Pamola on August 20, 1849. The Keep party copied the note and returned it to the bottle on the summit. When they returned, Marcus Keep, in a letter to the editor on September 1, 1849, announced that they had made a successful trip to the Baxter summit and found the note in a bottle on the summit of Pamola. The third party of women to reach the summit of Katahdin would not come until September 1855, when John Stacy would guide a party including five women to the summit.[29]

There were others who came to the area for its beauty, including scientists, artists and explorers. The most well-known artist who came to visit the area for its natural beauty was Frederic Church, of the Hudson River School of American Landscape painters; in 1852, he made the first of five trips to the area to paint the natural landscapes. A variety of scientists visited the area in 1861, including geologist Charles H. Hitchcock and agriculturalist Ezekiel Holmes, who traveled the area conducting their scientific research while surveying the natural resources of Mount Katahdin and the Wassataquoik Valley. In 1900, the botanist Merritt L. Fernald traveled the area, just as had his father, Merritt C. Fernald, president of the University of Maine, in

1874. Harvard professor Charles E. Hamlin visited in 1879, 1880 and 1881; during the latter trip, he persuaded Marcus Keep, then sixty-five years old, to accompany him one last time to the Great Basin, a great mount cirque on Mount Katahdin. There were also explorers who came to see what was there in the valley and beyond, such as the Katahdin explorer George Witherle, who based out of Lunksoos in 1889. In the 1920s and 1930s, Myron Haliburton Avery, the father of the Appalachian Trail, traveled the area, writing and collecting photographs about the Wassataquoik Valley and Mount Katahdin, setting down what would become some of the best recorded history of logging.[30]

Perhaps the most famous visitor in the early years was Henry David Thoreau, who made three trips to Maine in 1846, 1853 and 1857, following ancient Wabanaki canoe routes through vast, primitive wilderness. His trips are well known, and much has been written about the trips and his guides. During the first trip in 1846, he climbed Mount Katahdin, traveling by way of the Penobscot and West Branch of the Penobscot River with his guide Joe Attean; the trip was recounted in an article called "Ktaadn,"

George Witherle with his two guides on their 1899 expedition to Mount Katahdin from Lunksoos. *Myron Avery Collection, Maine State Library.*

published by the *Union Magazine* in 1848. His second adventure came in 1853, when he traveled to Greenville and then down the West Branch of the Penobscot River to Chesuncook, returning by the same route with Joe Attean as his guide, later published under the name "Chesuncook" in 1858 by the *Atlantic Monthly*. His third trip in 1857 was by far his longest, taking him to Chesuncook and onto the Allagash Lakes, then down the East Branch of the Penobscot River to Bangor with Joe Polis as his guide. The third article, "Allagash and the East Branch," did not appear in print until after his death.[31] In 1864, the trilogy was published under the name *The Maine Woods*. His last essay has been suggested as the trip where Thoreau's wilderness ideology matured into a vision.[32] The book was widely read by travelers, serving as an introduction to the world of the great wilderness adventures available in northern Maine. The book has inspired generations of people to travel to explore the headwaters of the Penobscot River and climb Mount Katahdin.

On his last trip, Thoreau would travel with his friend Edward Hoar, with Joe Polis as his guide. In the beginning, Thoreau had a low opinion of his guide, assuming that he would be a somewhat limited resource.[33] What he did not realize was that Polis had served as the tribal representative to both Augusta and Washington, D.C.; he was a tribal shaman and friends with Daniel Webster. Thoreau not only would employ Polis as his guide but also wanted him to act as a mentor in the ways of the Penobscot culture. Polis believed in the unseen powers and knew the advantage of controlling those unseen forces,[34] which is one of the things Thoreau would learn about Polis. In Thoreau's journal, he spent only about a tenth of the journal on more than a quarter of his trip, perhaps indicating that he wanted to get home and out of the wilderness. The last leg of Thoreau's wilderness adventure would begin at the 1847 log crib at Matagamon Dam—not the dam there today, but rather one just upstream that has now been replaced by the current concrete dam built in 1941. It was here that they were made to walk along the shore while Polis paddled the canoe through the rapids below the dam. Thoreau was surprised as he stepped ashore within a few feet of the river, where he expected unbroken wilderness; what he found instead were the marks of the loggers where they had cut trees, appearing all along the river. Their first riverside campsite below the dam was on a gravel bar near a large bend in the river about four miles below the dam. This site would become known as Checkerberry-Tea Campsite, where they stayed on the evening of July 30, 1857. Thoreau wanted something different for supper to drink, so his guide used his knowledge of wild plants to brew some tea from the small riverside plant called checkerberry. The area is called the Oxbow area, which would become a favorite location of the artist Maurice "Jake" Day, who was best known for his work with Disney Studios and his creation of the character Bambi.

After supper, Polis showed Thoreau how to write on the underside of birch bark while he cooked a moose tongue and lips for the next day's lunch. The next day, they came to what was called Grand Falls, as the individual pitches had not yet been named. Here Thoreau had to go along the shore through thick forest; when he complained to Polis, Thoreau was reminded that as a ten-year-old boy, Polis had made the same trip while destitute for food, which generally served to silence Thoreau for a short time. Thoreau found it strange how regular Polis was about having comfortable meals, as if he had an internal clock guiding his meals. Once below the falls, Thoreau described very little about the river until they came to a set of large animal tracks in the mud alongside the river in its bank. Polis told him they were the tracks of the Indian devil cat or cougar, which was really better known as a wolverine.

The woodland creature's name was Lunkxus, a corruption from Native American language, which was later change to "Lunksoos" in stories. The creature was a feared by the Abenakis for its fierce defense of its territory. This left a strong impression on Thoreau, and the name would later become the name of the camp just downstream from the location where they had seen the tracks. At this point, it had been an extremely long day for them, as they had to walk along the edge of the stream for half of the day. They camped on the east bank of the river across from the month of the Wassataquoik Stream on a steep, high bank near the old road. Here he began to figure out the selection of the campsite made by Polis—the high bank, with its breeze, was good for a bug-free sleep. The next morning, they headed downriver and quickly reached the Hunt Farm. It was here that he had planned on a second ascent of Mount Katahdin, but the combination of travel time, wanting to get back to civilization and Edward Hoar's sore feet would prevent the climb from taking place. The two sports were extremely excited about reaching the Hunt Farm to purchase more block sugar, as they had used their five-pound supplies purchased four days earlier on Chamberland Lake and needed more. But to their disappointment, the farm was closed, with only a few farmhands gathering hay. So, while the Hunt Farm was one of the most important outposts on the river, Thoreau did not say much about it in his journal.[35]

While Thoreau's essays about his wilderness travels would become the introduction for many to the meaning of nature and wilderness, he was unwilling to listen to the stories associated with the names that were so important to his guide. Here is the major difference between Thoreau and his guide. Thoreau was a visitor to the wilderness, developing his definition of nature, while Polis just saw it as an extension of his home. For Polis, returning from a long trip into the woods was no different than returning home from the store. It wasn't only Polis who had a difference of opinions with Thoreau—Ralph Waldo Emerson[36] read the eulogy at Thoreau's funeral, criticizing his writings in a most uncharitable manner considering the occasion. Emerson and Polis had opinions of nature that were completely

This March 1879 photo of William Sewall (*left*), Wilmot Dow (*center*) and twenty-one-year-old Theodore Roosevelt (*right*) was taken before heading into the wilderness hunting. *Theodore Roosevelt Collection, Houghton Library, Harvard University.*

William Wingate Sewall (*left*) and Wilmot Dow (*right*) were both from Island Falls and had built a reputation as outdoorsmen. *Theodore Roosevelt Collection, Houghton Library, Harvard University.*

different from the views of Thoreau. There are those who today still have the views of Polis, with very little concept of what wilderness and nature mean, whereas many others view it as a place to visit[37] and then return to home to civilization just as Thoreau had viewed it.

One of the most important national visitors to area came in August 1879. A sickly twenty-one-year-old Theodore Roosevelt[38] would make a trip into the wilderness with William "Bill" Sewall, his guide from Island Falls. Sewall was the first nonnative person born in Island Falls and lived in the nicest house in the community, one that was always open to visitors. Roosevelt had been to Island Falls before using Sewall and his younger nephew Wilmot Dow as his guides. Earlier, Sewall had taught Dow the ways of the woods, but soon the student would become the master. Dow was to become the area's best shot and would become a better all-around guide. Judging by the way the men lived and dressed, you would think that they were simple-minded, uneducated hillbillies, but in truth, William Sewall, though simple in many respects, was a lover of nature and well versed in poetry. Theodore Roosevelt was a lover of nature and reading as well. One thing he liked about Bill Sewall was his size and look—he reminded him of one of his heroes from literature, a frontiersman who could do no wrong in the wilderness. Roosevelt was well aware of the writings of Thoreau and the geologist Charles Hamlin.

The famous trip to climb Mount Katahdin would start on August 26 with a rough ride in a buckboard to the Hunt Farm. The party was made up of Theodore Roosevelt; William Emlen Roosevelt, a cousin; Arthur Cutler, his tutor; Wilmot Dow; and Bill Sewall, his guide. At the Hunt Farm, they would leave the buckboard, cross the river and then head up the Wassataquoik Stream toward Mount Katahdin. While crossing the Wassataquoik a second time, Roosevelt lost one of his boots, but he would not give up, making the trip in a soft-soled moccasin he carried to use as slippers in camp. Both of the guides figured it would just be a matter of time before young Roosevelt would give up on the trip, but he pushed on to Katahdin Lake. As they made the push to climb Mount Katahdin on August 29, starting well before daybreak, Roosevelt complained about his feet, as the rocks were unforgiving compared to the soft forest floor. But he pushed on, making the summit, while even his friends were turned back by the difficult conditions. He was very pleased with himself and felt that he was cut from the same cloth as his guides.

While returning to the Hunt Farm, both of the guides became lost in the tangle of cutting roads leaving Katahdin Lake, which made Roosevelt realize that they were just men who were very comfortable in the woods and nothing more. Their return trip took them to the river, which they crossed to the waiting buckboard and a long, rough ride back to Island Falls. Bill Sewall from Island Falls and young Teddy Roosevelt would become lifelong friends during this trip to Mount Katahdin. Roosevelt would remember the trip with great satisfaction and pride in later years.[39] Some Roosevelt scholars feel that it was this trip that started his realization of the importance of wilderness and its protection.

There were two early visitors to the area who produced a great amount of information about the early years along the river: the artist George Hallowell and the explorer Myron Avery. In 1903, Hallowell came to the wilderness seeking physical recovery. He became intrigued by the log drive on the Wassataquoik and spent time carefully documenting each and every step of the log drive. He recorded sixty-two glass negatives of the drive as he followed the loggers. This was the first and perhaps the best documentation of the historical operation up the Wassataquoik Valley. During his trip, the great wildfire of 1903, a rapidly moving forest fire, pushed him out of the

Wassataquoik Valley to seek refuge across the East Branch of the Penobscot River at the Lunksoos Camps where he was staying.[40] He barely escaped that wildfire but did manage to save the glass plate negatives showing life on the river. Myron Avery had the same type of love for the area, and his ability to collect early information about the history allowed him in his writings to paint a picture of the hardships and drive that the early loggers had to remove the timber; in many cases, his writings were the only record of the early logging history of the area.

Protecting the area's resources for the people of Maine was the goal of Percival Baxter, one of the most influential men to work in this area. While on the train coming home from the Republican National Convention in Chicago, Baxter and the other Maine delegates heard lumberman Burton Howe of Patten extol the virtues of Mount Katahdin as the place to form a park. So, in 1920, Percival Baxter of Portland took his first and only trip to the top of Mount Katahdin, guided by Burton Howe and the famed mountain guide Leroy Dudley. It would be from this trip that he and others

Percival Baxter and his group crossing the river in a bateau from Lunksoos Camps. This August 1920 expedition to Katahdin would be used to promote a proposed Mount Katahdin State Park. *Baxter Collection Maine State Library.*

would advocate that the state create public parks from unproductive land. The influential group of explorers comprised Percival Baxter, the president of the Maine Senate at the time; Arthur Staples, editor of the *Lewiston Evening Journal*; Leroy Dudley, the famous Mount Katahdin guide; Burton Howe, the trip organizer; John Mitchell, the district chief fire warden; Willis Parsons, the fish and game commissioner; Charles Barnes, Speaker of the Maine House; and George Houghton, Bangor and Aroostook Railroad representative, as well as others who would stay at Lunksoos before their trip to discuss issues.

The trip would lead to Baxter's proposal to create Mount Katahdin State Park, which would one day become Baxter State Park.[41] The party had traveled from Patten to Lunksoos Camps, where it would then cross the East Branch of the Penobscot River in a traditional river bateau on August 6, 1920, beginning their expedition to climb Mount Katahdin. They followed the Wassataquoik Tote Road, turning off to Katahdin Lake while following the same route that Theodore Roosevelt used to climb the mountain.[42] From Katahdin Lake, they followed the 1916 AMC route to Chimney Pond and on to the summit using a variety of routes. Howes suggested that for the area to become a park, the Great Northern Paper Company would have to be on his side and the land should be owned.[43] GNP continued to purchase lands before others could; in February 1920, the maps of a proposed park were given to the legislature. The bill to create Mount Katahdin State Park provided for the establishment of a board for the project. While the majority of Maine's people favored the formation of a park, the major industrial forces were strongly opposed; in 1921, the GNP began extensive logging east of Katahdin up into the basins. In 1928, the president of GNP died, and the new leader of GNP, who was much more friendly to the idea of the park, agreed to the sale of Mount Katahdin to Baxter on November 12. Baxter continued the efforts to purchase lands and encouraged others to contribute to his cause; on March 3, 1931,[44] he formally donated the parcel to the State of Maine on the condition that it be kept forever wild. Today, you can still see Percival Baxter's words at Katahdin Stream Campground: "Man is born to die, his works are short-lived. Buildings crumble, monuments decay, wealth vanishes. But Katahdin, in all its glory, forever shall remain the mountain of the people of Maine."[45]

There is one last visitor who captured the imagination of the American public. His adventure came at a time when the American people needed a hero during the Great Depression. The visitor was a young boy of twelve from Rye, New York, named Donn Fendler. He became lost in 1939 while on a Katahdin climbing trip with his family—including Donn's father; Donn's twin brother, Ryan; his younger brother, Tom; Henry Condon; Fred Eaton; and family friends. On July 17, 1939, Donn and his friend Henry, bored with the group's pace, went on ahead. The boys were excited about exploring the tablelands, but a mountain storm moved in suddenly, locking everything in a thick fog; Donn panicked, leaving his friend as he tried to run back to the group using a shortcut. In his panic, he lost the trail, wandering the tablelands and hoping to find his group or the trail. But as he wandered in the wrong direction, he became completely separated from his party during the storm. Being lost in the mountains in a storm is one of the worst things that can happen to an inexperienced hiker.

Donn's disappearance launched a massive manhunt that involved more than 350 searchers, with headlines splashed across newspapers nationwide. As the days passed, hope of finding him alive waned, while the search and hope became front-page news across the country. Donn spent nine grueling days wandering alone, hungry and bruised, struggling over Mount Katahdin and then down off the backside to the Wassataquoik Stream. In his travels, he followed the stream and finally the telephone wires downstream along an old tote road, passing several abandoned and falling-down lumber camps along the way. He finally made it to the banks of the East Branch of the Penobscot River, having lost most of his clothes; across from Lunksoos Camps, the camp manager's wife spotted Fendler collapsed, clothed only in his white underwear but waving across the river for help. Fendler was rescued covered in bug bites, dehydrated and sixteen pounds lighter than when he started his ordeal. He was brought across the river by canoe, where his parents were called, and he was cared for at the camps before heading downriver to Grindstone by canoe. He fully recovered and was lauded for his courage and persistence at a time when Americans needed that kind of hero. He credited his survival to his Boy Scout training, remembering to follow the stream downhill to civilization. He was honored with a parade and an article in *LIFE* magazine. He even met with President Franklin D. Roosevelt, where he was presented with the Army & Navy Legion of Valor's medal for outstanding youth hero of 1939. Joseph Egan wrote a book with Donn Fendler's help titled *Lost on a Mountain in Maine*, which quickly became a children's classic. It was a tale of Donn's struggles, things he saw or didn't see and how he lost most of his clothes.[46] The ordeal was going to be honored in 1941 with a trail following his route from Katahdin to Lunksoos, but other factors came into play and the trail was never built.

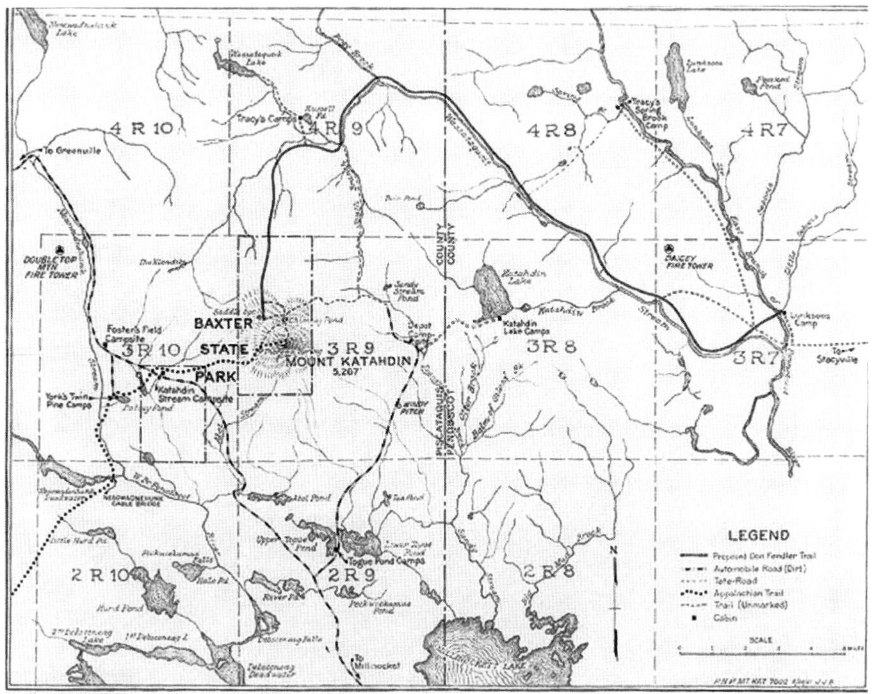

In July 1939, twelve-year-old Donn Fendler became lost for nine days on Katahdin when thick black clouds engulfed him. The map shows his route and a proposed hiking trail. *Myron Avery Collection, Maine State Library.*

While Henry David Thoreau was a visitor, it was his book *The Maine Woods*, a series of essays, that would define wilderness and the reason to explore the forests of this area for the country; for many readers, the book was the introduction to the meaning of nature and wilderness. The accounts of Thoreau's travels were the most widely read information about the Maine woods for many years to come. The writings have inspired countless generations of travelers seeking to experience nature by traveling the woods and waters as Thoreau did long ago. While the Penobscot below Medway has changed dramatically since the times of Thoreau, the river, lakes, streams and hills to the north are largely unchanged. In many ways, there are fewer people in those woods today than there were during the lumber boom when Thoreau traveled the river. The woods and waters that Polis traveled are still an important part of the Penobscot Nation's ancestral homeland for traditional activities, but now they also provide wilderness tourism for many other people.

CHAPTER 2

ROADS INTO THE WILDERNESS

In the Provisions of the Separation in 1819, which paved the way for Maine to separate from the Commonwealth of Massachusetts, the states agreed to an equal division of public lands of Massachusetts within Maine. The lands were to be split evenly between the two states[47] to support the separation. So, on March 15, 1820, when Maine became a state, it immediately formed the Maine Boundary Commission, which authorized a joint survey expedition. Maine hired Joseph Norris to lay out the boundaries of these unallocated lands between the two states, starting with a survey from the boundary marker that had been placed at the headwaters of Monument Brook going from the New Brunswick Border in the east to the Quebec Border in the west (the border was still being contested with our neighbors to the north); this line would become known as the "Monument Line." Once the survey was completed, the lands were quickly sold off to wealthy land barons in the Bangor auction; often the lands would change hands several times in one week or even more than once in a single day.

While the lands had been purchased, there was no real way to get to them until roads were constructed. The roads that were constructed were not the roads that we know today but rather wagon roads that would barely allow for travelers to ride. Rough and rocky, they were used by settlers, scientists, explorers, loggers and recreationalists coming to the area. Access would become an issue, but the difficulties over the northern border with Great Britain would lead to some help. In 1828, a military post was established at Houlton, and the Military Road from Bangor to supply the post was

The first Bangor and Aroostook locomotive to go through Sherman Station and Stacyville in late October 1893. *Stacyville Town Office.*

completed in 1832. The traveler heading north would follow the Military Road at Molunkus, where the Aroostook Road (1830) was constructed, to Stacyville and then finally to the military post at Fort Kent. Railroad travel did not reach Bangor, about sixty miles south, until 1855; did not reach Mattawamkeag until the European and North American Railroad in 1869; and did not reach Stacyville (organized on July 21, 1860, from the township T3 R6 WELS and Davidson, now a ghost town) until almost fifty years later in 1895.

But long before that, William H. Hunt had built a farm (T3 R7 WELS) along the river to service lumbermen and explorers. In 1835, he cut a rough winter road to Stacyville to bring his family into the wilderness.[48] This was perhaps the first road in the area, which would have been followed by a road joining the Hunt Farm and Dacey Clearing to haul supplies and boards. This area of Maine was very remote and considered to be wilderness when in 1839 Hunt and seven other landowners petitioned the Penobscot County commissioners for a county road to open the area to settlement. The petition stated that "a county road is much wanted...for opening a communication from the East Branch of the Penobscot River with the Aroostook Road…there being no public communication whatever with the waters of the East Branch." The petition also suggested that there were large tracts of excellent selling land lying between the Aroostook Road and the East Branch—"locating a road through it will facilitate settlement… and increase the value of the land through which it may pass. We therefore pray that a road may be located commencing near William Hunt's on the East Branch and running easterly until it intersects the Aroostook Road where you in your wisdom may see fit."[49]

A county road was again proposed on January 28, 1852, to the commissioners of the counties of Penobscot and Aroostook, who met at the Patterson Tavern on the corner of the road to Hunt Farm and the Aroostook Road to take up a petition by James S. Stacy and eight others. Their road started at the Patterson Tavern near the southeast corner of T3 R6 WELS (Stacyville), very close to the Aroostook Road and traveling up over the Kelly Hill for about nine miles to the East Branch of the Penobscot River at the Hunt Farm, making only one bend at the town line, located at the edge of T3 R7 WELS, where there was John Stacy's halfway house.[50] In 1855, James Stacey and thirty-four others went to the Supreme Judicial Court, which found the 1852 road to be defective, so it used the original location of the 1838 road. There is evidence that the 1838 road was laid out by a surveyor because it went straight to the town line for the Hunt parcel and then turned due west to the river. While it does not say, one would have to assume that the county road followed the road roughly cleared by William Hunt. It was at the Stacy halfway house that the road split to go to Hunt Farm or follow the Mountain Tote Road to Lunksoos. There was another road petition in 1874 by William Gillchrist and four others to make minor changes to the road, but the road's position today reflects only those minor changes[51] and has remained the same over the years.

The Hunt Farm has changed hands a number of times, finally being sold in 1881 to Chauncey R. Patterson. He connected the two farms by a better road along the river.[52] The road would eventually be connected to the present-day Happy Corner Road in Patten in 1903. The road that goes along the river between the two farms today is the same that was constructed in 1881. As the road became less used, it fell in a state of disrepair; in 1939, when Donn Fendler's father came by the Stacyville Tote Road, he described it as being extremely rough, as it was used only by logging trucks. In a visit in 1939 by a small group of boys setting out to fish, they described having to walk into the river; the road was so rough that the trip could not be made

Madison Tracy Farm at the beginning of the Stacyville Tote Road heading toward Mount Katahdin. *Lucius Merrill Collection, Bangor Public Library*.

The Rogers packhorses going through the road from the end of the Happy Corner Road, past Lunksoos Camps, headed for the river crossing. *Myron Avery Collection, Maine State Library.*

any other way.[53] With time, the road would be improved, becoming the main road and being renamed the Swift Brook Road, as it crosses the Swift Brook where there was once a small community.

Once the roads into the east side of the East Branch of the Penobscot River reached the river in 1835, the loggers were soon fording the river.[54] The first ford was located near the Hunt Farm, as there was a long section of shallow river; the second ford was just above Wassataquoik Stream, and in time there would be a cable ferry at the Dacey Clearing.[55] The two fords crossed the river and joined near the mouth of the Wassataquoik Stream, which would become the start of the Wassataquoik Tote Road. The Wassataquoik Tote Road was constructed by lumbermen in 1841,[56] going up and over the south flank of Deasey Mountain to avoid the steep forested canyon on the lower Wassataquoik Stream; then it continued along the edge of the north side of the stream until it reached the large moraine,[57] a location where the glacier had dropped a great many boulders, forming Orin Falls. That was as far as the road went for a long period of time. Then, as the value of timber climbed, the road would continue up along the north side of the stream, traveling through rough country covered with boulders.

Today, the road can still be followed where the men moved the boulders to the side of the road or blasted them. This was the same road used for logging operations in the long log spruce operations that began in 1883 with Tracy and Love. As they worked their way westward, they cut all the white pine and spruce trees that they were able to cut, floating them down the Wassataquoik into the Penobscot and on to Bangor. In 1841, they stopped at Orin Falls due to the massive moraine crossing the area from south to north. The lumbermen moved back downstream a bit to where they developed what would become called the Lower Katahdin Crossing, allowing them to cut timber on the south side of the stream. The Lower Katahdin Crossing was the first location moving upriver on the north side where the conditions of both water depth and smooth gravel bottom finally came together to allow a safe crossing; in the early years, the crossing allowed logging to taking place on both sides of the river moving outward. What gave the crossing its place in history was when the Reverend Marcus Keep, in 1846, would use this crossing as he pioneered his trail to explore Katahdin after he first climbed the mountain.

All those who explore the area should recognize the name of Reverend Marcus Keep. He was born in Swanton, Vermont,[58] studied in Middlebury College and graduated from the Bangor Theological Seminary in 1846. He started out as a missionary to the wilds of northern Maine from Burlington to

Above: Loaded packhorses crossing Hot Brook Bridge just before the Lower Katahdin Crossing on the Wassataquoik Tote Road. *Myron Avery Collection, Maine State Library.*

Right: Reverend Marcus Keep was the wilderness guide who blazed the first trail up Katahdin. *Myron Avery Collection, Maine State Library.*

St. Francis, covering a distance of more than one hundred miles from 1847 to 1850, finally coming to Ashland, where he remained for the rest of his life. Keep wanted nothing more than to live in close communion with nature, while caring little for the conventionalities of society.[59] He made his first attempt to climb Mount Katahdin in 1846 with James Haines, leaving from the Hunt Farm, from which they crossed the East Branch of the Penobscot and then the mouth of the Wassataquoik, where they joined the road up the Wassataquoik Stream. They forded the stream using the Lower Katahdin Crossing and then followed rough logging roads as far as they could before heading cross-country by compass to the Pamola summit and the Katahdin mastiff. He blazed and cut the trail to Katahdin Lake where it was only five miles to the base of the mountain. In the spring of 1848, he cut the final section to the east side of the mountain near Avalanche Brook. He tried to get others to help him, but few were interested in the project; only his friend John Stacy was willing to help. June 1848 was the opening of this first trail up the east side of Mount Katahdin.[60] On his 1846 trip, Marcus Keep felt that he had visited the "court of God" and wanted to make it possible for women to visit the mountain. The trail quickly became the favored entryway to the Mount Katahdin region, starting from the east side of Mount Katahdin with a visit to Hunt Farm. In recognition of the work Reverend Keep had done in establishing the trail to Mount Katahdin, on February 19, 1859, the Maine legislature gave him two hundred acres of land at the outlet of Katahdin Lake, where he hoped to build the Katahdin Mountain House, a grand hotel for explorers. Marcus Keep continued to guide trips using this route until 1881, when he finally settled down in Ashland, Maine.

Continuing upstream by the 1850s, the search for the massive pines was no longer important, as the loggers would start cutting eight-foot pine for boards.[61] When Foster J. Tracy and his son-in-law, Hugh Love, from St. Stephens, New Brunswick, arrived in 1881 to cut long log spruce for the new owner, T.H. Todd, Foster's men began the task of rebuilding the road and preparing the stream for an 1883 river drive. As the lumbermen continued to push the road inland, they ran into another moraine that slowed the progress. At this point, once again, they went downstream a bit looking for a shallow, boulder-free section and developed another crossing to access the timber on the south side of the stream. This crossing would become known as the Upper Katahdin Crossing, used not only by lumbermen but also by explorers headed for Mount Katahdin.

In 1876, a group of scientists from Boston formed the Appalachian Mountain Club.[62] Then, in 1886, Maine guide Clarence Peavey was hired by

The roads followed the path of least resistance and often looked more like trails than roads, but they would manage to take loaded wagons. *Lucius Merrill Collection, Bangor Public Library.*

a group to create a road from the Wassataquoik Streams to Katahdin Lake to be used as a base for climbing and exploring Mount Katahdin.[63] The rough road/trail was needed because the earlier Lower Katahdin Crossing and Keep Trail had been completely destroyed in 1884 by a wildfire.[64] The route that Peavey cut was called the "Appalachian Trail"—the trail named almost fifty years before the present-day iconic long-distance trail from Georgia to the summit of Mount Katahdin that was laid out in the 1930s. The trail started at the Upper Katahdin Crossing, where the "Nine Mile Camp" was located on the north side about one mile below Robar Brook, and traveled to the north end of Katahdin Lake. This crossing was used because the Tracy and Love lumber operation had developed it for the logging on the south side of the stream, the site of the Lawler Camp, where today there are still a large number of artifacts.

The route itself consisted of linked logging roads with a few sections cut and marked in between to connect the roads. When constructing the trail, Peavey followed the roads used by the Tracy and Love operation to the Green Woods, a section of forest not burned in the 1884 wildfire. Leaving the Green Woods, Peavey cut the trail heading toward the northwest corner of Katahdin Lake. He cut the trail through an area known as the "Blowdowns," where a few years earlier Patterson, the owner of the Patterson House, had been lost for a number of days while returning from a Mount Katahdin climb. The blowdowns were caused by a storm on November 12, 1883, known as the "Maine Cyclone." The trail, which was considered to be a wagon trail, entered a bog, giving the first exceptional close-up views of Katahdin. Peavey's trail from Upper Katahdin Crossing to Katahdin Lake became known as the "Appalachian Trail." In 1916, the AMC had another August Camp at Mount Katahdin, utilizing an improved trail system cleared for it by Madison Tracy crossing at Upper Katahdin Crossing.[65] In 1920, this was the crossing used by Percival Baxter, who then followed the Tracy Trail to the summit of Mount Katahdin.[66] While this trail was not used for very long as a hiking trail, it does show up on the 1930 USGS map of the area, which indicates the importance of the trail/crossing and its location to exploration in the region.

By 1883, Tracy and Love had finally reached the headwaters of the Wassataquoik Stream, deep in the heart of what would become Baxter State Park. Once the park became established, the state would construct a game warden cabin just outside the boundary of the park near the mouth of Townline Brook on the edge of the road in order to protect the wildlife. In 1919, after fires and floods caused damage to the roads, camps and dams, logging in the area would came to an end. The road became known as the Wassataquoik Tote Road, which in 1941 was proposed to become the Donn Fendler Trail, as it was the road Donn followed reaching Lunksoos after being lost for twelve days in 1939.

One of the more interesting but less known routes to Mount Katahdin that traveled through the Katahdin region in the early days was the short-lived road called the Sandbank Trail. In the 1920s, with all the rumors swirling about efforts for a future park in the Katahdin region, either state or national, people were becoming excited about the business it would bring to the area. This was a time when development of the area as a park seemed very possible, with hotels in the Katahdin Lake area being proposed. So, in 1920,[67] a Stacyville resident named Madison Tracy, who lived at the start of the Swift Brook Road, blazed and cut a new trail just to the south of the Hunt Farm to the south shore of Katahdin Lake, where there were sporting camps.[68] The trail follows and takes its name from Sandbank Stream, the name of the stream being derived from the glacial delta that formed 13,900 years ago as the glacier retreated, with the water flowing into the ocean,[69] located near where it now enters the river. The trail started at the Hunt Farm and traveled downstream along the eastern edge of the river until just below Whetstone Falls, where it crossed the river in a shallow section. The trail then followed along the Sandbank Brook, crossing it several times and then over the ridge tops to the west before finally reaching Katahdin Lake.

The purpose of the trail was to position Stacyville, which had good railroad access, as the gateway community to the future park should it materialize. The Great Northern Paper Company was strongly opposed to not only the concept of a park but also this route because it wanted access to the forests to be from its mill and its town, Millinocket.[70] The GNP pushed its road into Basin Ponds from Millinocket, opening access to recreational activities from the south. The new road, coupled with extensive logging operations in the area of the new trail, soon destroyed the Sandbank Trail. Despite attempts to keep it open and cleared from the logging operations, it never became established as a route to the future park. With a change of circumstances created by the new GNP road, the Sandbank Trail went from a possible highway to the future park to an obscure woods trail that had all but vanished by 1928 when Myron Avery made his trip to the area.

In Patten, there was a gristmill that was purchased in 1867 by William Gifford, who converted the mill into a sawmill[71] that would be purchased Edwin and George Merrill, becoming the American Spool Mill. The citizens of the town of Patten, in 1894, voted to pay Bangor and Aroostook $15,000 for the laying of a track between Patten and Sherman, as well as for the construction of a train station. By 1895, the mill needed more birch to make spools, so it constructed a road to the highlands to the west, where there was a good supply of birch along the river. In March 1898, thirteen

The old tote roads still look very much the same in the winter, even though this photo was taken well over one hundred years ago. *Myron Avery Collection, Maine State Library.*

independent thread and yarn companies merged to form the American Thread Company, and the road that it constructed would become known as the American Thread Company Road.[72] The road was constructed to Kimball Brook near Bowlin Pond, maintained and used by Paul Gagnon until the late 1930s, when it was described to be in very poor condition. The road left the rail station going out Water Street to the north of Wiley Pond, crossing the Seboeis River near the mouth of Moose Brook and on to Bowlin Camps on the East Branch of the Penobscot River, where there was a fish hatchery and a number of upper-river sporting camps. The road today is the entrance to the eastern section of the monument known as the Grondin Parcel.

In the north, access came from what was called the Matagamon Tote Road (Route 159 today), the road traveled from Patten to Shin Pond, with the good road stopping at the Crommett Farm. According to an 1851 map of Penobscot County, the farm was owned by Aaron Scribner and operated as a lumbering depot/farm on the road to the wilderness. The farm is found just past the Mount Chase town line in T6 R6. Aaron and two of his sons died in a tragic fire. In about 1900, the farm would become known as the Crommett Farm, owned by Samuel Crommett, and it was a major hub of

The roads through the wilderness often did not last very long due to logging, spring floods and heavy harsh winters. Here you have a bridge, but just downstream you can see what is left of an older bridge. *Bert Call Collection, Special Collections, Raymond H. Fogler Library.*

activity in the early twentieth century.[73] The farm was used until 1944, at which time it was abandoned; it finally burned in 1966. Now all that remains is a sign designating its original location, a foundation and artifacts around the area just west of the town line.

The Town of Patten petitioned the Penobscot County commissioners in 1906 and again in 1915 to build a road to the Matagamon Dam on Grand Lake.[74] The petition was denied both times, the commissioners using the argument that the road would benefit Piscataquis County more than Penobscot County, which would be shouldering the financial burden; also, the lumber company representatives were opposed to the project because of the taxes involved. The Grand Lake Road, which is now Route 159, was constructed by the Civilian Conservation Corps.

The CCC was a federal work-relief program launched in 1933, one of several programs known collectively as the New Deal, President Franklin D. Roosevelt's farsighted response to the national shame and despair of the Great Depression. From 1933 through 1942, the CCC provided government-paid public works. Most projects were aimed at developing and conserving the nation's parks and forests. Originally for young men ages eighteen to twenty-five, it was eventually expanded to ages seventeen to twenty-eight.

The Crommett Farm was the last stop for the explorers and loggers headed into the northern part of the monument. It offered supplies for the traveler. *Patten Lumbermen's Museum.*

Route 157, which was constructed in 1933 by the CCC, still offers the same view of the mountains today as you approach the monument's north entrance. *Bert Call Collection, Special Collections, Raymond H. Fogler Library.*

After physical exams and conditioning, recruits were assigned companies in project camps for a minimum of six months and a maximum of two years. The men earned room, board, clothing and a solid monthly paycheck—the base pay of the "CCC boys" was thirty dollars per month, of which twenty-five dollars went to the enrollee's family.[75]

There were four camps in the Katahdin area working primarily to connect a road between Greenville and Patten. The 130th Company Project 52 was under the supervision of the National Park Service, the 193rd Company Project 61 was under the supervision of the National Forest Service, the 123rd Company Project SP-4 NP was under the supervision of the National Park Service and the 159th Company Project 60 was under the supervision of the Maine Forest Service, which was located in Hay Lake. The function of the Hay Lake Camp was to work on the construction of the wilderness roads from Patten toward Greenville, as well as trails and fire protection lasting from June 1933 to September 1937. The Hay Lake Camp was the longest-lasting and best-developed camp, even having a recreational beach on the lake. If you drive by the location of the Hay Lake Forestry Station, you would never realize it was once a thriving work camp. Today, all that is left are artifacts of a camp water-heated woodstove, several chimney stacks, foundations and other associated items.[76]

One road that was never built but planned and surveyed was the Katahdin Road, a road from Stacyville to the summit of Mount Katahdin. In the 1850s, a road to the top of Mount Washington was constructed that is now the oldest man-made attraction in the country.[77] Its success was amazing, with people coming from all over the world by train to go to the top of the mountain and see the surrounding mountains. With the construction and operation of other mountaintop roads in 1856, Shepard Boody petitioned the Maine legislature for a road; the petition would allow him and his associates to construct a turnpike road from some point on the Aroostook Road[78] to the summit of Mount Katahdin. The petition also would allow him to collect tolls, but the road had to be constructed within three years. He had built a reputation working for Amos Roberts and the Strickland brothers (owners of a large tract of land in the Allagash headwaters) as a logger/engineer when he devised a way to get Chamberlain Lake to flow against its natural current. Boody proposed the raising of waters in Chamberlain Lake via a dam and then the digging of a canal across the low height of land between Telos and Webster Lake to restore the pre-glacial flow of the Allagash to the south.

Shepard Boody, the great wilderness engineer who reversed the flow of water in the Allagash, making it flow to Bangor. *Patten Lumbermen's Museum.*

The road charter was approved on April 9, 1856, by the Maine legislature for a company consisting of Shepard Boody and others.[79] He had to follow the most convenient route to Mount Katahdin, which would start in Stacyville. In 1858, Boody employed the J.W. Sewell Company of Old Town to make the survey for the road. The survey started on November 1, 1885, with David Haynes as the chief surveyor, Marcus Keep as the guide and chairman, Charles Lyons as second chainman and Thomas Haynes[80] as the axe man. The surveyor kept all measurements and angles for the survey; the chainman used the two ends of a measuring chain[81] to measure the distance, while the axe man marked the trees along the way. The survey was presented and accepted by the state on March 28, 1859. The survey crossed the East Branch of the Penobscot River close to the site of the Lunksoos Camps.[82]

The battle for future recreational sports played out in the legislature when on February 19, 1859, Marcus Keep was given a two-hundred-acre lot at the outlet of Katahdin Lake, where he planned to build his Katahdin Lake House, a grand sporting camp, to serve the clients coming to climb the mountain. He was given the land in consideration of the services and money used for keeping a trail open from the East Branch to the Summit of Mount Katahdin. After Shepard Boody filed the results of the survey of March 28, 1859, he petitioned the legislature again and was granted the use of ten acres for twenty years where they planned for another grand hotel. The petition was granted on March 30, 1859, under the condition that a building would be constructed within five years. Because of conflicts with Keep, Boody sold the Katahdin Road Company to William Dawson for $100. According to records, the Katahdin Road Company never complied with the conditions, and records show the grant never being made to it. In 1874, the land in T3 R9 was transferred to Francis Reed except for one thousand acres for the public use.

Why was the road never constructed? There are no reasons ever given, but one could guess. The remoteness of the area certainly was a factor, and logging operations were making it difficult to maintain roads; then there was the changing character of the country. The Civil War had just ended, and people were looking west for their investments. In contrast to the situation at Mount Washington, the railroad did not reach Patten, Maine, until the 1890s, more than thirty years after the route was surveyed. By that time, the Millinocket area was developing, and the access to Mount Katahdin was moving to the south. Many feel that it is fortunate that the road was not built; the mountain would remain a wilderness, and eventually the access to Mount Katahdin would come from the south. Had the road been built, the whole character of the region would be completely different.

There are several other important wagon/horse roads that were used for a short period of time but never lasted. The East Branch Tote Road followed up along the west side of the East Branch of the Penobscot River from the river crossing to Little Spring Brook. The road was constructed in the late 1840s and fell into disuse when the American Thread Company Road made it to the river in 1895. In the 1880s, the battle for the best river crossing caused the Mountain Tote Road to be constructed from the halfway house on the Stacyville Tote Road to Lunksoos. The beginning of the road went through wetland and then down a fairly steep grade. In the 1920s and 1930s, William F. Tracy and P.A. Tracy of Stacyville operated sporting camps known as Tracy's Camps at the mouth of Little Spring Brook, where William Tracy ran pack trips into Baxter State Park via a wagon trail along the Little Spring Brook over the ridge and down Robar Brook and then up the Wassataquoik Stream.

The historical access also came from the rail side town of Davidson and the lakeside community of Matagamon, both of which are now gone. Matagamon lives on, not as a community but as part of the Boy Scout High Adventure program, still using some of the original buildings. Davidson, on the other hand, is gone. It was once a thriving community. Ora Gilpatrick was a Houlton businessman and president of a local bank who purchased the entire township and founded the town of Davidson in 1901. The town was located on the edge of a small lake next to the railroad. It was located in the middle of what was then six square miles of virgin forestland. This was a factory town owned by Gilpatrick, and he lived in the largest house in town; he also built homes for his two sons. This community had a log mill, a clothespin factory, a dairy, a station house, a blacksmith shop, a schoolhouse, a town hall, a store, a hall for movies and dances and two boarding homes for men and women. It even had wooden sidewalks along the main street to protect people from the mud. It had more than forty teams of horses hauling lumber from the woods daily when it was most active. After the stock market crash of 1929, the town was sold to a Maine senator, and the lumber industry in town started to fade.[83] This rail town was busy until 1931, when for some reason the town stopped being a town. Folklore indicates that the town did not have a church, which may have been the cause of it disappearing; either way, it has now slowly returned to nature.

The very important community of Stacyville had a population of 264 in 1870, and it had a population of 265 in 2010; while the community has not grown, it is still the gateway to the region. Today, there are three roads recommended by the National Park Service to be used to enter the monument by vehicles. While there are other roads, they are private, and it is recommended that they not be used due to logging operations and heavy truck traffic. These three roads are the same three roads that were historically used to access the wilderness. The southernmost road is off Route 11, the Swift Brook Road (once called the Stacyville Tote Road), which is considered to be the gateway to the southern portion of the monument and the Katahdin Loop. The entrance to the northeastern section of the monument, known as the Grondin Parcel, leaves Patten going out Waters Street; as the road changes from tar to gravel, it becomes known as the American Thread Company Road, still the same original road for this section. The road used to access the northern section of the monument is off Route 159, the road constructed by the CCC, out of Patten. A short distance after you cross the bridge over the East Branch of the Penobscot River, you will take a left turn, reaching the monument after a half-mile dirt road, the East Branch Tote Road. There are many other historical roads in the area used for lumbering, but today they are no more than ruts lined by boulders going through the forest, with a few that have become hiking trails.

CHAPTER 3

WILDERNESS DEPOTS

Shortly after Maine became a state in 1820, the "Monument Survey" of the area was completed and Maine started selling off lands that had not been sold by Massachusetts. The land in township T3 R7 was purchased by Edward Smith in March 1825. He then quickly sold the land to a group of gentlemen from the Gorham area as an investment for the sum of $2,781, or about twelve cents per acre in 1830, which at the time was a considerable amount of money. The group of men from Gorham included a physician, Elihu Baxter; a gentleman, James Smith; a farmer; and a merchant, Charles Hunt. In June 1831, thirty-one-year-old Charles Hunt sold his share of the land to his older, more adventurous brother, William H. Hunt of Carthage, who at the time was a thirty-nine-year-old farmer. Local folklore says that the land that William Hunt purchased was sold for one and a half cents per acre, which would have made the selling price considerably less than his brother originally paid for the land, but records show that he paid $1,200 for his brother's section along the river. The original purchase has an interesting connection that would play out in the future, as Elihu Baxter was the father of James Phinney Baxter, whose son, Percival Proctor Baxter, would become the face of Baxter State Park.[84]

Attracted by timber and cheap land in 1833, William H. Hunt and Hiram Dacey, his friend from Skowhegan, left their families and headed north, first going to Danforth and then on to Island Falls, finally following along the Aroostook Trail[85] to T4 R6.[86] William Hunt left his wife, Nizolla Gould of Dixfield, whom he had married in 1812, with their eight children plus one on the way to tend their Carthage farm. Local lore says that the men traveled by road from Stacyville to the East Branch of the Penobscot River, but there is no evidence of a road or trail going to the river at the time. It is more likely that they traveled from Patten, where in 1828 lumber baron Amos Patten of Bangor had purchased the land for timbering and started logging in the area just to the west of T4 R6, now known as Patten,[87] where he was working his way toward the Seboeis River. From Patten, the two men traveled west using Amos Patten's logging road into the wilderness until they reached the Seboeis River. It was there that William Hunt and Hiram Dacey constructed a raft to be used to float down the river to the East Branch of the Penobscot River, looking for the land and a place to settle in the newly purchased property. It would make sense that the men had the information from the journal of Jonathan Maynard, where he had noted two different locations along the river. The first was just downstream of the Seboeis River, where he indicated he had found hops growing in a field as if they had been planted in rows; the other location was on the east bank of the river about a mile below the mouth of the Wassataquoik Stream, where there was an expanse of relatively flat and fertile soil on a high bank overlooking the river.[88]

Just as they crossed into the land that had been purchased, there was a location where the land was relatively flat and fertile. Here Hiram Dacey would build his cabin and farm of the west side of Lookout Mountain, just a few hundred yards downstream from the current location of the Lunksoos Camps. It would come to be called Dacey Clearing; the stone foundation of the original home can still be found. Folklore says that he was able to build his cabin without using a single nail. By today's standards, it would not seem to be possible, but in his day, most wilderness cabins were built this way, using wooden pegs to hold things together. Not only did his location have land good for farming and raising cattle, but it also had two brooks that ran down the side of the mountain around his home for a good source of water.

William H. Hunt would continue downstream, past the mouth of the Wassataquoik Stream, to the location that Jonathan Maynard had noted in his survey journal. It would be this relatively flat and fertile location where he would build his farm. The stone foundation farm was constructed by workmen hired by Hunt. The farm consisted of a main house, several outbuildings and a large barn next to the house for the oxen and hay. One of the first visitors described the building as a one-and-a-half-story farmhouse with a kitchen and several fireplaces built of hand-hewn square logs covered with boards.[89] The men cut the trees on his lot to grow crops of hay, potatoes

The Hunt Farm was an outpost in the wilderness for travelers and also acted as a supply depot of both recreational users and loggers. *Lucius Merrill Collection, Bangor Public Library.*

and corn. They also had a sawmill using a whipsaw, a type of saw used to make boards that would be operated out of either a pit or a framework. It was run by two people, the pit man and top man, who worked the saw, which had angled teeth sharpened so that it would cut only on the downward stroke; on the upward stroke, the teeth were designed to remove the cut wood or sawdust. The top man had to deal with pulling the saw back up, which was backbreaking work, but the pit man had to contend with sawdust in his mouth and eyes, as well as the danger of being crushed by a falling log. Two men working together could produce up to three hundred board feet of wood per day. The men would also produce splints, boards split tree length, for covering the roof, attached using wooden pegs. The man-powered mill produced boards not only for the Hunt Farm but also for the Dacey Clearing cabin farther upriver.

These wilderness farms were considered to be the gateway to the region known as Wassataquoik Valley, leading on to Mount Katahdin and beyond. Most people at that time considered the location to be the limits of civilization—the last great unexplored wilderness in the East.[90] The farms were more like depots, established to support the logging industry, but they also soon would begin to serve recreationists, scientists, artists and others who wanted to explore the Katahdin region or climb its mountains. They even manufactured birch canoes for the explorers. The Dacey Clearing was also the last outpost in the wilderness to the north and was the last stopping place for travelers headed upriver into the Allagash region. The two farm buildings were constructed with the methods that they knew best: a stone foundation made of squared granite and a framed log building. The homes, outbuildings and barn would be referred to as post-and-beam construction today, where wooden pegs held them together. One of the early visitors in 1846, Everett Hale, admired the Hunt Farm for "picturesque beauty utterly unsurpassable" as it sat on a high riverbank overlooking the river and mountains to the west. The soil at the Hunt Farm was exceptionally rich, and in 1847, it produced seventy-five tons of hay to be sold to the lumbermen.

Once the farms were built, William Hunt returned to Carthage to bring his wife, Nizolla, and their nine children—Lois (nineteen), Charles (seventeen), John (fifteen), William (fourteen), Sarah (nine), Jane (seven) Clarissa (five), Abigail (three) and Oliver (one)—back to the farm; all would become involved in the operation at the farm.[91] Once at the farm, the family continued to grow, and in 1834, Levi Hunt was to be the first child born at the wilderness of Hunt Farm. Then, in June 1836, Joseph Hunt was born, bringing the wilderness family to eleven children. In the early years, the Hunt family not only sold boards and lumber but also were well known for selling salmon; their home served as a resting spot for lumbermen, explorers and sportsmen. The farm quickly became an important center for exploration and commerce for the region in the early years. To encourage travelers to stop at the farm, the Stacyville Tote Road passed by the Hunt Farm wells; as the traveler came down the hill, just before the farm beside the road there was a nice well for travelers to get a drink of fresh water, and just beyond on the other side of the road was another, much larger stone well for animals. The stone edge to the well prevented the animals from standing in the well but still allowed them to drink the water easily. The children would regularly travel to town in the summer to sell the crops or salmon. They used seine drift nets that were close to one hundred feet long to catch the salmon, which came up the Penobscot to spawn. Some of the salmon were huge, and the small children could only carry one at a time into town to sell.

American author, poet and philosopher Henry David Thoreau, during his third trip to Maine in 1857, canoed past the location of the Hunt Farm on July 31, 1857, in search of sugar. The cabin would have been there, but he did not mention it in *The Maine Woods*, only talking of the fact that there were men gathering hay and other crops in the distance. He did camp about one mile upstream, near the mouth of the Wassataquoik Stream. He described in his book, seeing the tote road along the east bank of the river, which was the road between the Hunt Farm and Dacey Clearing.

According to folklore, the Hunt Farm was a dry location, but it is rumored that in the early years, for weary travelers, William Hunt kept a number of barrels of rum in a taproom downstairs for his guests. The story goes that one day, when nobody was around, he went down into the cellar and sampled one of the kegs, perhaps a bit too much. The next morning, he awoke with a nasty hangover. So, he was all done selling rum—if it made people feel as he did, it was wrong and he didn't want anything to do with it. He took the kegs outside, picking up an axe and smashed in the head of each barrel, letting the contents run out on the ground. From then on, the Hunt Farm was a dry hostel for travelers.[92]

Life in the wilderness was difficult for the family of thirteen; living from May to October at the farm, the Hunts, growing two crops of hay and a fall crop of potatoes, would soon become exhausted. The winters were harsh, cold and lonely along the river, so they began to retire to their new house in

The wilderness depots grew hay and potatoes to supply the logging camps. They were successful because they were built closer to the lumber operations. *Pattern Lumbermen's Museum.*

Stacyville for the frigid winter months. On December 7, 1842, Nizolla died. Not long after her death, he remarried to Deborah Hunt, but it was never to be the same for William Hunt. In 1848, William Hunt sold the farm to his son William M. Hunt for almost twice what he had paid for it per acre and moved into Stacyville.

During this period, not much is known about the Dacey Clearing, as it soon would become abandoned, with rumors indicating that Hiram Dacey was not happy with all the traffic and moved farther into the wilderness. The homestead was taken up by a hermit named Israel Robar, who would live in the cabin for a number of years as a squatter, moving farther into the wilderness when the lands changed hands in 1881.

William M. Hunt continued to manage the Hunt Farm until 1874, when it was sold to Chauncey R. Patterson, a tavern owner operating on the corner of the Aroostook Road in Sherman. His tavern was also the stagecoach stop along the road, and I am sure he was aware of the business that Hunt was doing at his wilderness farm, outfitting travelers and the logging companies, as the farm was used by loggers because of the shallow water and because wagons could ford the river easily. He also realized the possibilities for the location from the visitors to his tavern at the head of the road.

Perhaps the grandest of the expeditions that went through the Hunt Farm under his management took place in September 1877, when the American Landscape School used it as its base for a forty-two-day expedition to Katahdin Lake for exploring the Katahdin area and painting. The farm would be the point where artists would meet their five guides at a cost of about $650 each. They carried more than 800 pounds of supplies, including 180 pounds of potatoes, 80 pounds of sugar, 100 pounds of fish, 65 pounds of beans and assorted other items, including 8 pounds of lemons for their tea.[93] Frederic Church was so pleased with what William Hunt had to offer that he had him build a twenty-eight-foot canoe that was four feet wide and weighed 300 pounds to carry supplies. Church had purchased four hundred acres on Millinocket Lake with a view of Mount Katahdin to continue to paint. But as time went by, Patterson would let the Hunt Farm fall into disrepair to the point that it was falling down.

IN 1881, SIMON B. Gates purchased the Hunt Farm from Chauncey Patterson because the buildings were falling down. Gates had built his reputation as a top-notch hotel owner, building the Katahdin House in Winn in 1874, then the largest hotel north of Bangor. The three-story hotel was located near the rail depot and acted as the regional stagecoach office for those heading north. In early 1881, Gates purchased another large three-story hotel in Mattawamkeag at the mouth of the Mattawamkeag River along the Penobscot River; under Simon Gates's management, it became a very well-managed hotel,[94] located not far from where the Aroostook Road branched off the Military Road. His plan was to tear the Hunt Farm buildings down, remove all materials and use the clearing to build the first large hotel, which he called the Matagamon House. In the purchase, Gates had Patterson agree to not use the upriver buildings for loggers or sports while Gates was building a new hotel. The Matagamon House was a grand affair, located on a bluff above the river, looking west at the mountains. It had two full stories, with a large roofed porch. So, Chauncey Patterson moved upriver, leasing the Dacey Clearing, realizing its potential for a center of lodging for those going into the wilderness. He immediately began to construct a better road connecting to two wilderness farms.[95] He corduroyed the road, laying logs perpendicular to the road to protect the base, which was then covered with river-washed gravel, making it a solid, all-season road that could be used in early spring.

It was at this time that Chauncey Patterson would construct a road from the halfway house on the Stacyville Tote Road directly to the clearing; it was called the Mountain Tote Road because it passed the western face of Lookout Mountain.

In order for Patterson to abide by his agreement with Simon Gates about how he used the Dacey Clearing, the lease forbade the use of the camps for sporting business on the premises, so Patterson moved a bit north. The northern half of the township was owned by Dr. Charles Adams of Bangor, who in 1883 leased the land to Luther Rogers for lumbering. Chauncey Patterson was allowed to build a new guest house just over the property line in 1885 that he called the Patterson House.[96] The guest house was nothing special, just an overnight stop for travelers. By 1895, the old Dacey cabin had decayed to the point that it had to be torn down, leaving the stone foundation as a reminder of the past activity. The new location and road would have shifted exploration of the lumbermen and sportsmen from the Hunt Farm to the Dacey Clearing. Patterson's business continued until 1891, when Fred Ayer and Luther Rogers leased the facility from him as a headquarters for their logging operation up the Wassataquoik Stream. They renamed and rebuilt the Patterson House, calling it the East Branch House, which continued to operate for recreational activities in the area.

Major changes came to the area in 1894, when the railroad reached Sherman and Stacyville, increasing access to the area of the East Branch of the Penobscot and Wassataquoik. The rail service also expanded the popularity of the camps, even with the final part of the trip to the camp being made using wagons over rough roads. In 1895, Colonel Luther Rogers, a Civil War veteran from Patten, built an elaborate log sporting camp complex called Lunksoos Camps. These camps were managed in addition to the lumber operation. Henry David Thoreau described in his book seeing the tote road along the east bank of the river but not the camp. While traveling down the river on July 31, they ran across what his guide described as very recent tracks of an Indian devil or cougar.[97] The book was widely read during that period by people wanting to experience the wilderness. The story of the tracks may well have been the source of the name for the camp, as the name *lunksoos* is the Algonquian word for "Indian devil" or "catamount," which refers to a wild beast that terrorized native people and was said to be heard screaming in the valley by travelers to the area.

It was the era of great sporting camps, where travelers could stay overnight, get a home-cooked meal and hire a guide, bringing the comfort and safety of home to the wilderness.[98] The hotel was a grand affair that stood three stories high. The first floor had a surrounding open porch looking at the river out front. The second floor also had a porch, with a view of not only the river but also Mount Katahdin itself. The first and second floors were for the guests, while the third floor was primarily used for workers and storage. At the very top of the building was a sitting area with a 360-degree bug-free view of the surrounding lands. The building had the word *Lunksoos* spelled out using birch logs for letters on the front.

In 1892, due to increased business and promotion of his location, Rogers built a cable ferry that was used to carry sports and logging equipment across the river. It was a simple system, with a cable attached to trees on both sides of the river that could be removed during the winter. This cable was used to pull a flat raft for people wanting to cross the river; it was in operation until 1922, when it was finally removed. The Mountain Tote Road came directly down the side of the mountain to where the ferry was located. The ferry could carry a full team of horses and their load across the river in just a matter of minutes.

In 1901, the Ayer and Rogers Operation ceased the ownership of Lunksoos, which then reverted to Dr. Charles Adams.[99] In 1903, George Hallowell, the Boston artist, was hired to follow the logging operation up the Wassataquoik, documenting it in photography; he was chased out of

The Lunksoos Camps was a grand affair built in 1895 by Colonel Luther Rogers, a Civil War veteran from Patten, on property leased from Dr. Charles Rogers of Bangor. *Pattern Lumbermen's Museum.*

The Lunksoos Camps was constructed so that the kitchen was on the end of the building, and it had a place on the roof to sit and relax in a bug-free environment. *Pattern Lumbermen's Museum.*

The Nearest Large Camp to Mt. Katahdin

IS THE

Lunksoos House : :

at the Ferry, Penobscot East Branch, 8 miles from Patten.

Close by the famous Wissataquoik river, and surrounded by splendid trout ponds. Here deer are abundant and moose plenty, and there is ideal canoeing on river, streams and lakes. **The Lunksoos House** offers first-class accommodations in every respect; is an especially desirable resort for families; has private lodges and also string of camps on the Wissataquoik trail which are the only camps at the north spur of Katahdin. Daily mails. Trains met. Guides, teams and saddle horses furnished.

Ride to Katahdin

The only saddle trail in to Katahdin basin starts from the Lunksoos House, following the Wissataquoik valley, passing Katahdin lake and south end of Turner Mt., crossing Sandy stream, rounding the head of Sandy pond, and then climbing up roaring brook to the South basin, where a comfortable camp is located. The easiest, most picturesque way to visit Maine's greatest mountain.

Prompt attention given all requests for circulars or special information. Address

L. B. ROGERS & SON, Patten, Maine.

Above: This was the cable ferry, located just downstream from the Lunksoos Camps. The ferry was built by Rogers's crew and operated from 1892 until 1922. *Myron Avery Collection, Maine State Library.*

Left: When the railroad finally made it to Stacyville, the B&A started a magazine to bring people to the camps using the train. This ad for the Lunksoos House appeared in the 1905 editions. *From* In the Maine Woods, *B&A, 1905.*

The river ford was located at the Hunt Farm and used in low water; there also was a ford downstream from Lunksoos Camp. The solid gravel bottom was used to safely cross the river by wagon and horse. *Lucius Merrill Collection, Bangor Public Library.*

the forest by the great wildfire of 1903, barely making it across the river and seeking refuge at Lunksoos. The full-page advertisement in the 1905 edition of the Bangor & Aroostook magazine *In the Maine Woods* shows the importance of the sporting camp. While the 1903 wildfire was stopped by the river, the grand hotel called Lunksoos did burn to the ground in 1908. The camp was rebuilt in 1910 by Dr. Charles Adams and Edwin Rogers of the Ross Lumbering Operation, which began promoting the saddle trips to the Great Basin and beyond. The new lodge was very similar to the lodge that is currently at the location. It was a two-story affair with a large porch for relaxing. This would also mark a turning point for the camps. The Matagamon House started going downhill around 1900 because the town of Patten voted in 1894 to pay the Bangor and Aroostook Railroad for a rail station in town. Also, the road to Lunksoos would be through the Happy Corner Road, so no longer would visitors to the area have to travel by the Stacyville Tote Road past the Hunt Farm.

The Ross Lumbering Operation held the Lunksoos lease, continuing to push the roads deep into the mountains. The camps were once again leased in 1920 to Edward Draper to be used for his pulpwood logging operations. Draper continued to operate the camps until late 1930, when Nelson McMoarn took over the lease, operating the camps for recreational purposes. The era of the great sporting camp was quickly coming to an end, perhaps in part due to the automobile, which gave people the ability to travel and greater freedom to take short vacations. In the mid-1950s, the camps once again burned and were replaced by the lodge that stands there today. The lodge was leased to private parties for their personal use. The camp was purchased in the 1990s, when the cabins were added to the property for use by hunters. The camps were opened to the public as sporting camps in 2003, gaining a reputation for bear hunting in the great north woods.

The Matagamon House passed through a series of different owners. After the big 1903 wildfire, the Matagamon House was leased by Tracy Madison from Simon Gates, and Tracy lived at the start of the Stacyville Tote Road. According to an advertisement in the 1912 edition of *In the Maine Woods*, Irving E. Palmer became the proprietor of the establishment. In his advertisement, he reported the uncommonly large salmon and trout to entice fishermen.

After the flood in 1919, the Matagamon House started to see increased use for a very short time, but by 1944, it had been abandoned and was falling into disrepair on the bluff above the river. Nate Hudson, who had taken up residence in the Palmer home, finally tore down what remained of the Matagamon House in 1951. The wood was used to build a fence for his garden.[100] The remains of the small cabin used by Nat Hudson were finally claimed by the river in the late 1950s, when the Matagamon dam owned by Bangor Hydro had to release a large amount of water into the river; when added to the spring flood, this washed away the sandy bluff with the remains of the buildings. Today, all that remains of this once important hub of wilderness activity are two wells, barrel hoops, cans, wire fencing and other small items. With even such a short stay along the river, William Hunt's legacy still lives on today, from the name "Hunt Farm" to a number of local families' names such as Gould, Boynton, Rice, Rush and Morse, as well as the name Hunt itself. On April 15, 2011,[101] Roxanne Quimby purchased the 13.8-acre Lunksoos parcel, which included a lodge and four cabins, from a Florida couple,[102] to be used as an artist and writer retreat. With the 87,500 acres east of Baxter State Park designated as Katahdin Woods and Waters National Monument, Lunksoos Camps could begin to serve as a work center for the monument.

CHAPTER 4

WASSATAQUOIK STREAM'S IMPORTANCE

The Wassataquoik Stream and its valley have played a significant role in the lumbering history of the Northeast for a number of reasons: the remoteness of the area in the 1800s, even into the 1900s; the extreme difficulty in removing the timber to markets in Bangor; and the distance from supplies for the men and their camps. More often than not, the life of the logger working in the valley has been romanticized, but it was anything but easy. They led incredibly difficult lives in the wilderness forest, full of danger and hardships, with many losing their lives. Most of the logging was done in the winter, when the temperatures were cold and the snow deep. In order to get to the timber, they had to build roads through areas that had experienced heavy glacial activity, building wilderness camps as they pushed westward to get to the timber. Once the timber was cut, they had to get it out of the forest, which required building dams to control the flow of water for the river drives. Not only did they have to build dams, but they also had to remove the glacial boulders blocking the streams, sometimes using dynamite. The men would enter the forest in the fall to prepare the roads, clear the streams and cut timber, often with only one set of clothes. They would work hard all winter into the early summer, finishing with the river drive; by the time they paid the company for their room and board, they often would have little money to take home to their family.

When Maine became a state by separating from Massachusetts in 1820, part of the agreement was to share the unsold public lands in the northern part of the state, which meant sharing the rich timberlands. Because both states were badly in need of money, the money would come from the land buying boom in Bangor, when speculators purchased large tracts of land for pennies per acre at the auctions. The State of Maine was able to finance the building of the new capitol with the sale of ten townships of land in one day. It was set up so that each township had one square mile of land to support the public school; even though most townships had no people, they were planning for the future. Oftentimes lands would change hands several times in a single day. But the real push for timber in the valley would come with the panic of 1837, which was a financial crisis that touched off a major recession that lasted until the mid-1840s. Profits, prices and wages bottomed out, while unemployment skyrocketed.

Why was the Wassataquoik Valley the last great frontier for early logging in eastern United States, and what made it so special in the first place? In Maine, the first logging was done along the coast, and then the men worked their way inland. In 1820, the northern lands were opened, and the St. John River Basin, the Allagash River Basin and much of the Penobscot River Basin quickly became an industrial forest. Wassataquoik Stream flows from a remote, wild area in Baxter State Park known as the Klondike. From the point at which the Wassataquoik leaves the park, it drops more than five hundred feet in about fourteen miles of continuous boulder-filled rapids to its confluence with the East Branch. It is joined in its wild tumult by Twin Pond Brook, Katahdin Brook and Deasey Brook on the southwest and Robar Brook on the northeast, all increasing the flow.

The first road into the area came in 1841 with a ford that crossed the river either at the Hunt Farm or Lunksoos, joining shortly after and headed upriver. In 1846, when Edward Everett Hale and William Francis Channing traveled the road, they found a number of lumber camps along the way.[103] Very little is known of this period because no timber was delivered to the boom in Bangor. The men realized that to drive the stream would be extremely costly and difficult. When they reentered the stream in 1881, the loggers found piles of eight-foot-long pine timbers left in the river, blocking many of the side channels, that had been left high and dry to rot when the drive was hung up years earlier trying to drive the timber down an uncontrolled and obstructed waterway.[104] In 1881, timber baron T.H. Todd from Milltown, New Brunswick, purchased the timberlands to the west of the East Branch of the Penobscot. The manager for his operation was a St. Stephens, New Brunswick man named Foster J. Tracy, who along with his son-in-law, Hugh Love, was able to use the old 1841 Wassataquoik Tote Road, which was still in good condition, to move upriver. But what they found made them realize that it would not be as easy as they thought.[105]

The Tracy and Love operation, with their crew of Canadian loggers, headed up the Wassataquoik Stream in 1881 to prepare the stream for the 1883 river drive. They were sent to clear the glacial boulders (some the size of a house) from the streambed, build dams to hold the water and construct lumber camps where necessary. Todd spent $40,000 and used several tons of dynamite to remove the large boulders, straighten the channels and control the water. This would be the first recorded use of explosives to alter the Wassataquoik Stream. Sadly, he also lost six of his men in the process of preparing the stream.[106] Due to the high elevation, slow-melting snow and lack of large headwater lakes, the Wassataquoik was notoriously unpredictable and would often abruptly rise or fall several feet in just one day's time. Todd's intent was to cut long log spruce and drive them downstream to the city of Bangor, which already had claimed the title of the lumber capital of the world and was one of the busiest shipping ports, where he would sell his timber. The lumber would then travel to as far away as Australia and Chile, with the bulk of it going to Europe.[107]

The loggers generally started from Lunksoos Camps because the Hunt Farm had just changed hands, and while it had been repaired, it was not open to public use; they would then move along the 1841 tote road, which was a very rough boulder-lined road. After crossing the East Branch of the Penobscot River, they followed the old road to where the Wassataquoik Tote Road rejoined the Wassataquoik Stream. This was just above a heavily wooded steep-sided gorge where the river made a sharp turn around a large rock outcrop on the south side of the river. This was a location where the long logs would become jammed and block the river. So, the Tracy and Love crew built their first dam at this location. It is difficult to determine the origin of the dam's name. It is spelled Dace Dam, Daisey Dam, Deasey Dam, Daicey Dam and Dacey Dam in old logging articles, while the USPS 1953 Stacyville map has it spelled Deasey Dam, which brings us to the reason for the name. Deasey Dam would make sense because it is located on the flank of Deasey Mountain, but in 1883 there was no Deasey Mountain on maps. A 1920 article in the *Lewiston Evening Journal* stated that the name of the dam was a monument to a drowned river driver named Daisey, but it would make most sense that the name would be Dacey Dam after Hiram Dacey, whose farm was used by the loggers to start their trips into the wilderness.[108]

What is now called Deasey Dam would become the first of twenty-three dams that the Tracy and Love crew would build on the Wassataquoik. Deasey

Deasey Dam, the first dam built on the Wassataquoik Stream in 1883, was a log crib dam with sluice gates. *Myron Avery Collection, Maine State Library.*

Dam was built in 1883 about three hundred yards from the Wassataquoik Tote Road using the rock outcrop on the southern side as the primary anchor. It was a log crib dam with four deep gates to control the flow of water, with two splash gates to allow the logs to be directed downriver where the drivers wanted them to go with the maximum amount of speed. There were also two additional cribs upstream for a log boom to direct the flow of the logs and the storage of floating logs. The dam was built in extremely low water by using notched logs in the form of a crib, which was then filled with rocks and gravel found nearby. The source of the gravel came from both sides of the river, as there is still evidence of an extremely large pit in the side of the esker to the south of the dam; on the north bank, you can still see evidence of several small pits used for gravel. The stream cribs were built in the same manner but were fifteen feet square, with a large chain attached to the bottom center and then filled with rocks and gravel. The chain in the center was attached to long floating logs connected to the upstream shore. These logs were to direct the timber floating downstream in the sluiceways. The sluiceways were narrow, ten to twelve feet wide, where the logs would be fed downstream by the rapidly moving water over the dam. This way, the logs would be moving as fast as possible in a straight line down the stream. The construction and operations camps were located next to the road on a flat section of land just uphill from the dam. Where the road came closest to the stream, they built their camp, which consisted of a number of buildings, a blacksmith shop and a supply building.

The early operations had a decidedly New Brunswick atmosphere, as many of the loggers were old acquaintances who had worked for Foster

Tracy before in southwestern New Brunswick. In the spring of 1883, Tracy started the task of cruising the forest for cutting. Within a year, the operation consisted of nine camps employing 270 men, 110 horses and 12 oxen; the main camp even had children, complete with a school and a teacher.[109] But the operation fell into disaster the first year when on November 12, 1883, a late-season hurricane known as the "Maine Cyclone" flattened much of the forest to the south and west of Deasey Mountain. The storm blew down most of the tall timber in wind rows so that much of the wood never reached the ground. Then, in the early summer, a second disaster struck. On June 29, 1884, a wildfire, started by fishermen to drive off bugs, broke out near Norway falls. The fire burned for four days before rains finally put it out. Once the smoke cleared, the men realized that several of their camps had burned flat, and the newly built dam was destroyed. They also lost more than twenty-two thousand acres of forest, consumed by the wildfire. The timber that had been blown down by the storm the fall before just sat there, drying all winter, making it excellent fuel[110] for the fire.

You would presume that these disasters might have slowed things down, but that was not the case with the Tracy and Love operation. They quickly rebuilt the dam, as well as most of the camps upstream that had been

The construction of a crib dam used logs piled and then filled with gravel found close to the dam. The dam would have a spillway for logs. *Bert Call Collection, Special Collections, Raymond H. Fogler Library.*

burned. Their operation came to an end in 1891, leaving behind a legacy of dam construction, as they had built almost all of the dams on the waterway. The operation was taken over by Colonel Luther B. Rogers of Patten and Fred W. Ayers, owner of the Eastern Manufacturing Company, who were now operating out of Lunksoos Camps. Fred Ayer and Luther Rogers leased the facility from Chauncey Patterson as a headquarters for their logging operation up the Wassataquoik Stream. They renamed and rebuilt what was then called the Patterson House, creating the East Branch House, which became their headquarters and a facility for lumber operations on the river. They rebuilt Deasey Dam, making it wider and higher to increase the flow of spring water.[111] They operated the dam and camps until they were taken over in 1901 by the Katahdin Pulp and Paper Company, operating under Nathaniel M. Jones. Disaster struck again in 1903, when a large wildfire destroyed all the camps and dams in the operation once again. The fire was started in the Matagamon area by a group of men putting in telephone lines.

In 1910, Edward Draper of Bangor became manager of the company and rebuilt the dam, once again increasing the size. When operations restarted, it was no longer for long logs but rather for four-foot spruce pulp logs. This made the drive that much easier, as jams became rare. The wood was also no longer headed to Bangor but rather to the Great Northern Paper mill in East Millinocket by way of the Grindstone rail loader. In 1915, another blow to the organization came in the form of a wildfire, which halted operations of the dam.[112] In the spring of 1919, after a heavy snow year, there was a quick melt; when coupled with the burned forest, the water could not be held back, and the dam was washed out once again, never to be rebuilt.

Little remains today of the once active Deasey Dam site. On the north side of the river, near where the road once was, you can find the location of the construction/operations camp along a flat rise a few hundred yards away from the dam's location. There is evidence of several buildings and associated items such as stoves, wagon wheels, barrel hoops and lanterns. From the camp, there is a road that goes down to the bank of the stream, passing a small gravel pit used to fill the crib for the dam. The road branches to the east before coming down to the river, and another small stone dam is found on a side stream, perhaps used as the water source for the camp and its workers. Near the streambed, you can still find the remains of two of the boom cribs, with bits of the crib still present as well as the boom chain that achored the logs above the dam. At the location of the dam itself, there are still crib logs in the north bank of the stream, as well as part of the wing dam going up the steep banking. Across the stream in the large rock outcrop, you will find spikes in the stone outcrop that held the dam in place. Moving directly south, you will run into the major gravel pit used to fill the cribs for the dam. There is also a series of snub cables on the steep banking going up toward the top of the esker used to supply the dam.

Just upstream, you will find Katahdin Brook, which flows out of Katahdin Lake entering the Wassataquoik Stream. There was an old tote road that followed up the brook to Katahdin Lake that was built around 1902.[113] In 1910, the Draper operation rebuilt the dam at the outlet of Katahdin Lake in preparation for the river drive. During the winter of 1912–13, the brook was cleared of boulders, many of which had to be blasted. The only mention of this being used as a route to Katahdin was by the AMC August Camp in 1916.

As you move upstream into the wilderness, the next set of camps was located on the north side of the Wassataquoik Stream at the location of the Lower Katahdin Crossing. At this location, there have been a number of camps, but perhaps the best known was the Parker House, named after the famous Parker House in Boston. It was built around 1883 by the Tracy and Love operation as a way-stop as they moved farther into the wilderness. The original camps included a large storage building, a blacksmith shop, several outbuildings and a large main camp. The location was a relatively flat low area next to the crossing. The camps were rebuilt in 1910 by Edward Draper and became the Draper's Swing Camps; with the spring ice out of 1912 and the ice jam that blocked the river in this area, the camps there were flooded and destroyed. Today, there is little evidence of the camps other than a few artifacts and evidence of a building's location.

Farther upstream, you come to where Nine Mile Camps stood on the high bank of the river. Later, this was the location of the Draper Halfway Camp. The camps were both on the north side of the river, while on the south side, a bit back in the forest, you will find the location of the Lawler Camps next to a small brook. These camps were at the location of the Upper Katahdin Crossing. Today, there is little left of any of these camps other than artifacts on the forest floor. The Lawler Camp storage building was in the back on a small rise next to a swamp, where there are a few old sleds spread on the ground.

Moving upstream, you come to Robar Brook, where the second major dam on the Wassataquoik was constructed. Robar Dam and Robar Brook, as well as the camps, were all named after a semi-hermit, Israel Robar.[114] The site of the dam and camps is located a little over a mile and half upstream

Draper Halfway House, built in 1883, was halfway between Lunksoos and Old Camp City, deep in the heart of Baxter State Park. *Bert Call Collection, Special Collections, Raymond H. Fogler Library.*

from Orin Falls and about ten miles from the East Branch of the Penobscot River. It is an area of the river that is wide and shallow, with swampy areas on both sides of the river. The spring log drives would hang up or jam due to the shallow water as they slowed and got stuck on the edges of the stream. The dam was constructed during the drive of 1883 using logs taken from the drive itself by the Tracy and Love operation. The structure was a long, low dam, with several gates used to float the logs downstream, hold water for the drive and then release the water with the logs. With the dam in place, it remedied the difficulty caused by low water at this location. There were a number of camps over the years at the dam's location.

The Robar Camps consisted of a number of building set up against a steep rock ridge. The first camps were called the "Halfway Camps," or Roger's Halfway Camps, because they were halfway between Lunksoos, Edwin Rogers's headquarters on the river and New City Depot in the heart of Katahdin lumber country. The Wassataquoik Tote Road ran right through the middle of the camps, giving them good access; Israel Robar was the early camp cook.[115] Folklore has it that Israel Robar had served the camps well for a number of years, so the lumber company allowed him to build a small stone foundation and cabin just upstream from the dam and camps near the month of the stream; he lived more or less as a hermit in the 1880s and 1890s.[116] Even so, he did like visitors.

Over the years, Robar had gained a reputation as a great hunter, adventurous explorer and outstanding storyteller. During the years he lived at the location, he and his dog, Kelly, were always welcoming travelers passing through the area, whether they came upriver or overland for exploring or hunting. His love of reading *Leatherstocking Tales* by James Fenimore Cooper, coupled with his own embellished adventures, made for entertaining campfire tales for his visitors.[117] His camp became a welcome stopping point for hikers coming from the Lunksoos upstream along the Wassataquoik Tote Road or McDonald Camps going overland by way of Robar Pond farther upriver while exploring the area. Hikers knew that whether he was there or not, they would be welcome to stay and visit. The Robar Camps were later purchased by the Ayer and Rogers Lumber Company and used as a depot for its lumbering operation, but by 1901, the camps had become abandoned. William Tracy of the Tracy Camps continued to use the overland route into the 1930s. It is speculated, from description and location, that the fallen-down remains of one of these cabins was found by Donn Fendler as he worked his way down the river toward his rescue at Lunksoos Camps.

Robar Dam and the camps were located in a large, flat area by the stream where floating timber always had trouble. *Gray Herbarium Library Archives, Harvard University.*

The Wassataquoik Stream had few lakes to hold the spring runoff, so often the dams would wash out, just to be quickly rebuilt. *Bert Call Collection, Special Collections, Raymond H. Fogler Library.*

Today, much of what was once home to various logging operations hides a few secrets of the past. On the south side of the stream, you can still see where gravel was removed to build the dam, the remains of the cribworks for the dam and a stone-walled section of the dam; on the edge of the river, you can still see the logs that were once driven down the river and used to make the dam in 1883. On the north side of the river, metal artifacts are located around where the end of the dam once was located and in open areas where the building once stood. Just up from the dam on the downstream side of Robar Brook, you can find the stone foundation of the site where Israel Robar had his cabin; there is also evidence of the stove and kettles at the location.

One more camp was on the stream and inside the monument, located at the edge of Baxter State Park near Townline Brook. It was a small log cabin, about ten feet by fifteen feet, with a single window for light. The cabin was owned by Maine's warden service and used by game wardens during their forays into the wilderness. While it was small, it allowed the game wardens a home while doing their required checking on the sportsmen and trappers in the area.

Myron Avery, the great explorer, perhaps said it best in 1929 when he noted, "The Wassataquoik of today presents a curious contrast. It is entirely deserted and abandoned….Bared rock, a burned soil, a scraggly growth of 'pople' and—the aftermath of two terrific fires—an old field or two, ruined dams and tumbling down camps and an overgrown road are the mute and unconvincing records of its story. From the wilderness to a wilderness again, another life cycle of the Wassataquoik is complete." The Wassataquoik Valley has indeed return to wilderness of years gone by.

CHAPTER 5

LIFE OF A LUMBERMAN

LIVING AND WORKING IN THE FOREST

What was it like to be one of these young men? To live in the remote logging camps and working the wilderness winter forest cutting timber? To better understand how the lumbermen lived, we will look at where they lived and how they worked. Why did they go to the forest to work in the first place? The men working in the woods went by a variety of different names. You often hear the term "lumberjack" used on TV or in literature to identify the men working in the forest, but this was not a term used in the Maine woods—they were simply referred to as "loggers."[118] The men who worked in the woods were there because it was the only steady work that they were able to find; many came from extremely large families or were immigrants looking for a new and better life.

Once the land was purchased by a rich land baron, they had to figure out what the land was like and how the value could be extracted cheaply. The first person hired by the land baron after purchasing the lands would be what we call today a timber cruiser or surveyor, a person who would go into the forest to determine the value of the timber and how it would be removed. The work took a large party to do the survey because in the early days, it would take time to determine the location for the roads and the camps for the men. There would be swampers used to clear the way, with teamsters to drive the wagons and men to take care of the horses; because of the size of the group, they had to have a cook and someone to set up camp in the party. The surveyor would have an assistant and someone to use the measuring chain, as well as someone to record information about the survey.

The surveyors' report to the owner would include a map, the value of the timber and recommendations for locations to build the roads, dams and camps. Most of the work done by surveyors was done in the winter, when the ground and swamps were frozen, making it easy to travel across.

The first camps were built for easy access to the timber and were relatively small, holding only a few men, perhaps up to a dozen. The camps were sometimes only a three-sided shelter, but soon small enclosed camps would appear. The camp foremen would select a site for the camp, and a crew would be given a task of clearing the land and constructing the camp. While the camp was being constructed, the foremen would roam the area, looking for the best places to cut timber. The trails would be blazed with an axe so the men could easily find the location. Once winter arrived, the men would begin cutting timber. The reason most of the logging was done in the winter was because it would be easier to transport timber using sleds that were being pulled by horse or oxen and then, in time, by tractor to the water's edge, where the timber would be piled for the river drive in the spring. The sleds were made of four runners attached to a body that would hold the wood. They discovered quickly that by having four runners, the sleds would move much more easily over the curvy iced roads. Once the day was done, they would return to their one-room camp. It would have been a rough affair made of logs cut within easy distance of the camp itself. They were generally square and fifteen to twenty feet on a side, depending on the timber in the area. The size was controlled not only by the size of the local timber but also by the size of the crew using the camp.

The construction was achieved with single logs laid horizontally; then they were notched on the corner to stay in place. In the early days, nails were not an option, so they would work the sides in such a manner that the cabin would grow in layers to a desired height. The logs would sometime be peeled, but more often than not, the bark would be left on because the camps would only be used until all the local timber had been cut. The logs were heavy, so there was no need for the use of nails to hold the layers together; if anything, wooden pegs were used. The gaps were chinked or plugged with moss mixed with mud to seal out the cold and wind. The roof was constructed with logs, which were then covered with evergreen branches followed by large sheets of bark or slats and split cedar logs. The roof would leak when it rained or when the snow would melt on the roof. There would have been a door with an overhanging roof to add a bit of protection for the men, as well as a storage area for cooking wood. While there would be a door, there would be no windows, as glass was difficult to bring to the logging camp.

A typical logging camp. The cooking area is in the center, with separate doors for the logging crew and the cooks. *Bert Call Collection, Special Collections, Raymond H. Fogler Library.*

There might be as many as twenty men staying in a larger camp. In the middle of the camp structure would be a hearth made of logs filled with gravel. The fire would burn day and night for both heat and cooking. As for the smoke, it would leave through the holes in the roof and walls of the camp. It's hard to imagine what it must have been like to breathe the air inside those early camps. In the early days, the men would sleep on the floor in a single row. The bed was often marked by a single log used to hold hay or boughs in place for the men to sleep on. They would go to bed in the same damp clothes that they worked in all day with their heads toward the wall; their body heat would dry their clothes out as they slept. These were extremely close quarters, but the work was hard and the men slept well. The fire would burn all night, helping to keep the building warm and the men's clothes dry. The only furniture that you might find in these camps would be three-legged stools or, if they were lucky, a deacon's bench cut from a tree—they would split a log with four branches still attached to be used as a seat. The men in the woods were always looking for these types of trees to make life a bit easier.

All the logs heading downstream to market were scaled (measured) and stamped (the logging equivalent of "cattle brands") to determined value

The camp building would house all of the men living in very close conditions, while the horses would have to live in a smaller building. *Patten Lumbermen's Museum.*

ownership. The stamping was done with a long hammer-like tool, with the symbol of the owner in the end hitting the log, marking its ownership for all to see at market. Due to the seasonal nature of the business, logging camps tended to be temporary and often moved from place to place[119] once the timber was gone and a new location was selected. The workweek was from Monday through Saturday, starting at 5:00 a.m., long before the sun would rise, and finishing around 9:00 p.m. every night.[120] At the end of the day, the loggers would return to camp in the dark for supper, which was usually meat and potatoes. After supper, they had to feed the animals, sharpen their tools, repair the skid trails and dry their clothes as best as possible. Then it was off to bed six days a week. Sunday was kind of their "day off," but by today's standards, we would never call it such. Sunday was the time to wash and disinfect their clothes in giant kettles of boiling water and then repair any holes or tears in their clothes[121] by mending them around the woodstove. Life in the logging camps was never easy, and each logger generally had one set of clothes for the season, so they had to take extra good care of the set. Men ate out of the frying pan or metal kettle, often all together. There would have been a hovel with a floor of hewed log to keep the oxen and horses off the ground. The hovel had a floor to protect the animal's feet from the cold, as there was no source of heat in the hovel. There might have been a third building for storage of food, hay and tools.

Once the camp was constructed and foremen had blazed the trails, the men went about making the road network needed for moving the timber. All

Men ready to go into the woods to work, carrying the tools of their trade. *Patten Lumbermen's Museum.*

the trees would be cut to a width of sixty feet for the main road, which was about eight feet wide, and then the surface would be scraped down to the ground. Often these roads were laid out along a brook for a source of water to ice the roads in the winter, while always trying to avoid obstructions and troublesome grades. Once the design of the road was in place, men unskilled in the use of an axe would grade the road using hoes, picks and shovels. The men took pride in their ability to build roads, and it was said that no crew on earth could build a road as quick and solid as a woods crew. Today, many of those old roads are still there, just overgrown a bit. After the main road was complete, the side roads would be cut, smaller but in the same manner. Then clearings would be made for the log yards and skidways; the road layout would look like a tree with all its branches. This whole network of roads might only be used for a few years before the camp would be moved to another location.[122]

By 1860s, there had been several improvements to living conditions for the men. Tar paper or roofing felt, which had been used in the gold rush, started to make its way into the woods. This allowed the camp to stay much drier in the rainy winter weather. Also, the hearth was moved to the end of the camp structure, where there would be a chimney of small logs above that had been lined with clay or mud to prevent it from burning. The floors were now hewed logs rather than dirt, and windows were added to bring light into the camp. The bed was moved up off the floor and was now a long raised bunk with a log bottom covered with boughs or hay. Twelve to fourteen men would live in the camp together in very close quarters. The "best" part of sharing that one big communal bed was that, in most cases, they shared the lice that were often present in camps. Imagine sleeping five people in a king-size bed—that will give you some idea what it would have been like to sleep in the camp. The bed often had only one blanket, a spread

A camp along the river for the drivers, holding their peaveys and caulked boots. The cook is in the center of the photo. *Patten Lumbermen's Museum.*

or quilt sometimes twenty feet long that was filled with cotton batting for warmth, so you wanted to make sure that you were not the one at the end of the bed. It is hard to imagine the pungent odor that was created when the men would hang their wet wool clothes and socks by the fire to dry after a great meal of beans.

At about this time, the woodstove would make its presence known in the camps. This would be a huge improvement over the open hearth used in the earlier camps. Often the camps would have two stoves, one at each end of the camp to keep it warm. In the camps, the animals (either horses or oxen) would live in their own structure called hovels—these three-sided buildings would turn into four-sided barns to protect the animals from the elements and store the hay for feed. There would have been a hovel with a floor of hewed log to keep the oxen and horses off the ground, as well as stalls. The next major improvement made to these small camps would be a cooking stove and chimney made of metal. By the 1890s, almost all of the camps had stoves that would be used for heating and cooking. Often the camp boss had his own little cabin—not for his pleasure but rather to allow the men to talk freely. The larger camps, often called "unit camps," even had a small building for the clerk and perhaps a small store where men could buy articles of clothing, hats, mittens or tobacco.

By 1900, the camps had become even more specialized, looking very much like the logging camps of today. These would be unit camps, which would feature buildings specifically for the men to live and sleep. Then there was a building to house the kitchen and kitchen staff, with tables and stoves for cooking; full barns for the animals; a building for hay storage and the animal keepers; a blacksmith shop to repair and the manufacturing of equipment; and a clerk's office, where records were kept and equipment stored. With the increased specialization came requirements for skills and increased pay. The men worked six days a week, and only the cooks and teamsters would be paid to work on Sundays.

By the 1910s, the single group bed had been replaced by individual double-tiered beds in the unit camps, while the single bunk remained in the company camps until 1929. As the crew became more specialized, the logger had different jobs. The cooks and their assistants were the highest-paid workers, but there were other specialized positions in the camps. The blacksmith and saw filers played important roles in keeping the tools sharp and ready for use. You had the teamsters and swampers, whose job it was to make the roads and trails; the teamsters also had to take care of the animals and transport supplies to the camp. The men cutting down the trees were

A group with what was called a jumper wagon, designed mostly for winter use but also sometimes used in the summer. *Patten Lumbermen's Museum.*

Men using a crosscut saw. Two skilled men could cut a tree down as fast as a cutter with a chainsaw. *Millinocket Historical Society.*

called choppers, sawyers or limbers, depending on their jobs. The men who worked in the yard were the sled-tenders and yard rollers, who piled the logs. There was the camp boss, who ran the camp, and the walking boss, who was in charge of a string of camps. Many camps even had a wood butcher, whose job was to make and repair things made of wood.

When the loggers were working the forest, they would cut trees using either axes or crosscut saws and skid them down to the edge of the stream. When the spring arrived, they would roll the trees into the water to head downstream—this was called the river drive. The logs were stacked so that when the single bottom-front log was moved, the whole pile would roll into the stream, making it extremely dangerous for the logger removing or breaking the log. They used a long pole to keep the logs moving and caulked boots (boots with short sharp spikes in the soles) and always carried a knife to cut their overalls if they got snagged. Imagine, if you will, walking on floating logs with your caulked boots, using your pole for balance while going downriver, hoping not to fall into the stream because you were unable to swim—such was the life of the logger.

Their life was hard, and the work was dangerous. Some would make it through the winter just to be killed in the spring log drive. In 1888, the skeleton of Charles Stewart of Little Ridge, New Brunswick, was found in a gravel bar several miles below the Orin Falls. He had drowned when a jam released at Orin Falls and he was unable to make it to shore. As with most of the loggers either killed or drowned during the log drives, he was buried along the edge of the stream near where they found his body. His burial site was marked with an inscription in a large rock along the edge of the Wassataquoik Tote Road. The great wildfire of 1903 burned so quickly and hot that many of the monuments to the river drivers were chipped by the heat and the inscriptions lost. There were other drivers who lost their lives in this area and whose graves marked by inscriptions on rocks along the edge of the falls; when the stream was straightened again by the Rogers crew in 1891, the rocks were destroyed.[123] For William Haskell, who was killed breaking up a log jam and buried next to where they found his body, he would have a rapid named after him. More commonly, the logger or driver was just buried along the edge of the river, with their boots hanging in a tree. Perhaps their name would be inscribed on a tree or rock by their friends, just to be worn off by the future drives and lost in time.

CHAPTER 6

MEALS FOR THE LUMBERMEN

CAMP COOKING

In the early years, the men in a logging camp would share the duties of cooking. There would be a hearth of some type in their cabins, where they generally would keep a pot of beans cooking at all times. In these early camps, the men would often work seven days a week, but more commonly they worked only Monday through Saturday. Their day starting before dawn, they would have breakfast, work all day in the woods, return long after dark and then make a dinner that often consisted of beans, meat and potatoes. According to folklore, the early men would take two thick slices of bread soaked in cooking fat or a thick slice of lard in between and wrap this in paper to keep in their pocket. While it may not sound good, it did keep them filled and gave them enough energy so they did not get sick, as least in the short term.

Before long, they realized that taking turns cooking and preparing food cut into the time that they could be cutting and moving timber to market. At this point, cooking at the logging camps became a specialty job done by one person with a number of helpers. If you look at the evolution of the cookstove, it will help to better understand the changes in the cooking at logging camps. The first cooking surface was a log square about four feet to a side and about one foot high. It was generally in the middle of the camp building. There was no chimney, as the building generally allowed the smoke to escape out through the cracks in the logs or roof. The first big advance was the addition of a real chimney, which directed the smoke to the outside. In the early years, it was just a cribwork of small logs coated in mud or clay to harden in the heat so that it would not catch fire. Then came the metal stove, small at first and then larger, with the ability to bake goods. The camps would change with the addition of a dingle between two buildings—a roofed section between the cooking building and the sleeping building that was used for the storage of supplies. Then would come the gas stoves; the kitchen building would have several stoves for both cooking and baking goods for the men.

The kitchen would become the absolute domain of the cook, who lived by two rules: there was no talking allowed during meal times and the men were only allowed to take twenty minutes to eat. The only talking that one might hear came from the cook, who barked out orders to the cookee, or someone might say, "Pass the butter." The logger would self-select his seat, which would become permanent for the season so that he always knew where he would be sitting, allowing him to get into the dining area as quickly as possible. When someone new came to the camp to work, they would have to wait until everyone was seated before they could find a space that would become their seat for the rest of the cutting season. At the end of the meal, often their metal cups would be left in an upside-down position in the same place each day so that they would know right where it was located for the next meal; it could be filled quickly with either coffee or tea. The point was

The cook at his station, preparing food for the men working near Deasey Dam—a pot for coffee, a reflector oven for bread and a pot for stew. *Patten Lumbermen's Museum.*

Typical riverside kitchen. Everything is handy, and there's not much room to spare; everyone stayed out of the area except the cook, as it was his domain. *Patten Lumbermen's Museum.*

to get the men in and out as quickly as possible to increase production, as the men were being paid to work in the woods, not eat and talk.

The camp cook could make or break a camp with his reputation, but on the other hand, if the men were not happy with the cook, he would not last very long. The cook's reputation spread quickly throughout camps, often bringing men to work for a camp with a good cook. The cook was generally the highest-paid employee in the camp and one of the few employees who was paid for working on Sundays. In the Great Northern Camps in 1920, the cooks were paid a wage of four dollars per day, almost twice what the cutters were being paid.[124]

As the logging camp evolved, the camp kitchen became more developed and played an increasingly important role in the camp. Early menus and food choices were limited in the woods. As various historians and memoir writers have noted, most cooks could prepare meat in a variety of ways for the men. The choices were limited: salted meats and salted or canned fish, depending on location; some frozen beef, as long as it was eaten before it spoiled due to lack of refrigeration (or, if they were really lucky, fresh deer meat or bear meat secured by the men); pork and beans; molasses; gingerbread; and tea boiled in a pot. Cooks might excel, drawing a following with their ability to bake breads, pastries and pies or even in the way they made baked beans. Richard Judd said it best in his 1989 book *Aroostook: A Century of Logging in Northern Maine*, "The art of camp cooking…hinged on the knack of preparing one thing in a number of different ways." One of the ledger books for Joab Palmer in 1880 shows that his camp, with 160 men and 80 horses, consumed an unimaginable amount of food. The initial order, which in most cases was their only order, had 270 barrels of flour, 135 barrels of pork, 300 bushels of beans, 2,000 gallons of molasses, 300 bushels of potatoes and 3 tons of beef. For the horses, he had purchased 110 tons of hay and 5,500 bushels of corn and oats.

The camp boss always hoped that they had enough food to last the season but not any extra. They always tried to supplement their supplies with whatever they could shoot or catch going to and from the worksite. Once they had the food and hay, it had to be transported to the camps and stored for the winter, which was monumental task and took place in the fall. The closer the supply depot to the camps, the easier it was to get the supplies, which is why the wilderness farms came up to the river's edge. One of the items that are found throughout the forest in the area where there were logging camps are barrel hoops. The metal rings were placed around the barrels to hold them together, as most of the food materials would come in barrels ordered by the camp boss. The presence of variously shaped metal barrel hoops would verify the location of an old camp. The standard food selection hardly formed a nutritious diet, but it kept the men in good health and kept hunger away while they were working. What made a good cook was his ability to use what he had on hand and prepare meals in a number of different manners so that the loggers would think they were having something new and unique for every meal.

Breakfast, the most important meal of the day, was served before the sun would come up and was the same every day in the early years. The men were summoned by the cook as soon as the meal was ready with either a bell or banging on a cooking pot. The breakfast table was a massive affair, often providing sourdough pancakes; biscuits and gravy; pork, sausage, ham or salted pork; fried potatoes; doughnuts; and beans and coffee or tea—it was by far the largest meal of the day. The men might also get baked rolls or leftovers from the previous evening meal. The breakfast meal of the logging camp lives on today in many greasy spoons and truck stops across the country as what they call the "lumberjack breakfast" or "woodsmen breakfast," which generally has a lot of everything that they make served on the plate. What most people don't realize is that this would not have even come close to making those loggers working in the woods happy, as it was too little for them to survive on in the forest.[125] The nutrition side of their diet must have been satisfactory, as they ate the food for five or more months and disease was never discussed. There has been research done on their diets, and there may be several explanations for the lack of scurvy in the men. Scurvy is a vitamin C deficiency generally associated with seamen and would have shown up in the men as a weakness in the arms and legs, but it is never seen in the literature, even when the loggers had diets similar to that of seamen for long periods of time. Some feel that the seamen showed more in the way of symptoms as all of the men left the ships all together. Some researchers feel that the loggers probably ate dried fruit that was never recorded as part of their diet, as it was just a snack. Camp cooks were known for adding lemon juice to just about everything they cooked, which also might have been the solution. Another suggestion is that dried plums were often substituted for apples or added to apples in pies. One researcher even suggested that the men realized the issue and ate black ants that were found to have fed on the needles of pine tree in the forest and were a rich source of vitamin C. Or perhaps they did suffer but recovered quickly once they returned to their homes and resumed a normal diet.[126]

By 1910, meals appeared to go through some major changes in most of the logging camps, with as many as three hundred men being fed at a time, three or four times per day, seven days per week. There were major changes to the way food was cooked and served in the camps, all with the purpose of getting the men fed and back to work as soon as possible. The first thing that happened was better accessibility in the camps. Men began to see fresh meat, vegetables, fruit, eggs, butter and milk—as the transportation to the source of food improved, so did the supplies coming into camps. No more were the days of only getting supplies once in the fall that had to last all winter long. The second major change that came was a greater variety of food, with different items every day—menus of weekly meals became the norm, so the worker would know what he was going to have for the meal. But still, the meals would always be the same from week to week, so the men often had their favorites to look forward to. The third change was baking. As the cooks often had extraordinary skill at baking with few ingredients, they were able to substitute what few items they did have to make the baked goods special. Their secret ingredients were often never revealed, to keep them special for the camp and the men.

The final change was where they ate their meals—a separate building was constructed for eating, where the men would sit down at a dining hall with tableware and table service for all.[127]

Reviewing a menu for a 1919 logging camp kitchen, it did look very much like a restaurant menu, with some exceptions. The largest meal was always breakfast, and soups were a main part of the field lunch. Let us take a look at the typical day plan from one of the old camp menus. Breakfast would start with cornmeal mush, rice pancakes with syrup, gingerbread, buttered rye bread, fried potatoes, sausage and coffee—remember the food had to be eaten in twenty minutes or less. For their lunch, which was often served in the forest, there was vegetable soup, boiled potatoes, turnips, beets, buttered rye bread, green tomato pickles, chocolate bread pudding and coffee or tea. For their evening meal, called supper, there was fish and potato chowder, buttered bread, graham gems, fried cornmeal mush, stewed apricots, oatmeal cookies, a cup of plain peanut butter and coffee or tea. The guidelines for meals were set by the U.S. Food Administration. Reviewing the menu, you can see that there was a limited number of ingredients used to make a wide variety of foods. The rest of the week's meal menu would have been similar in structure.[128]

Most of the cooks were men, but some camps did have both women and children living in them. Often the small children would have the job of getting water for the cook or collecting wood to start a fire. Imagine as a young child having the job of getting water for the kitchen and horses. You would go down to the well and fill a bucket and then fill a second bucket so that you could carry the water on a yoke. You would have to fill the water barrel in the kitchen and then fill the water trough in the hovel for the horses. Back and forth until both were filled—it would not take long for the children to become tough doing that chore. The older boys might even be lucky enough to get a job in the kitchen as an assistant or apprentice cook. The cook would have many assistants, generally known as "cookees." Often it would be a young child wanting to learn the trade and become a camp cook; they were the best assistants because they would do anything for the cook.

These young people generally made as much money as the cutters and often more, as they were also paid for working on Sundays. Among their duties was washing the dishes, keeping the cooking fire fed at a constant temperature and delivering meals to the men working in the woods. The noon meal would be prepared in the cook building and then taken to the men in the woods using a one-runner sled that looked very much like a dog sled but was pulled by the cookee. It would be loaded with the food, dishes

As the kitchen became more specialized, the cooks had to do what they could with limited supplies; breads, cakes and cookies were camp favorites. *Millinocket Historical Society.*

The young boy second on the left was a cookee and was allowed to bring lunch to and prepare food for a small remote logging crew. *Patten Lumbermen's Museum.*

The cookee would bring lunch to the men, build a fire and heat it up and then return with the dishes to be cleaned; notice the rack of metal cups. *Patten Lumbermen's Museum.*

and cups. Once the cookee arrived at the location of the lunch, they would build a fire to reheat the food for the men and then serve it. Once the men had finished their meal, the cookee would collect their dishes and cups to be taken back to the kitchen and wash them clean. If there was no snow on the ground, they would carry the food in buckets attached to a pole that would be carried over their shoulder to the men. The men lived by the same rules while eating lunch as eating dinner: eat quickly and get back to work. There was no talking, and they had only twenty minutes to eat their food. The food and coffee were served in metal bowls and cups so it would cool quickly, forcing the men to eat more rapidly and getting them back to work as soon as possible.[129]

There was another person in the camp associated with cooking called the "bull cook." The bull cook was not really a cook at all but kind of a handyman around the camp or a chore-boy around the bunkhouse or camp. The name was given because it had a better ring than "camp helper." Oftentimes if someone was injured in a logging accident, becoming unable to work, he was given the job to give him a sense of worth. Often the bull cook was a broken-down old alcoholic, a hopeless physically or mentally handicapped person or an individual who was somewhat simple-minded, having been removed from the farm and placed in the big woods. Bull cooks often had very specialized skills—some were exceptional fire makers, others were weather prophets and some were great storytellers or good with a song. Among their chores would be filling the wood box, filling lanterns, cleaning the sleeping area and even serving food to the men.[130]

The men worked hard, and while the taste of the food was important, it was the number of calories that kept them working in the forest. On those cold winter days, they would require a minimum of six to eight thousand calories per day just to keep them working.

CHAPTER 7

MOVING THE LOGS TO MARKET

RIVER DRIVES

In the early years of logging in the Wassataquoik Stream Valley, the problem wasn't cutting the timber but rather getting it to market. Equipment and techniques had to be developed to move the timber out of the forest downriver. In 1840, the majority of sawmills in Maine were concentrated in Bangor, Orono, Old Town, Milford and Bradley, while the small community of Patten was a major center for logging operations along the East Branch of the Penobscot River. Since wood floats, they realized that pushing the logs downstream would be the best way, but they still had to get the cut logs to the edge of the streams for their trip downriver. Then, once the logs got to booming grounds, they had to have a way to know which logs belonged to what company. It was easiest to cut the timber and move it to the edge of the stream in the winter across the snow and iced roads, while moving it downstream was best when the water was highest during the spring runoff or with the water held back by dams. They had to develop methods to make the spring runoff last as long as possible by building dams and clearing the streams. So, they developed methods for moving logs over the snow and a way to control the spring runoff that required special tools and techniques.

Let's take a look at some of the tools used by the men moving the logs out of the woods and down the river. The blacksmith was one of the higher-paid workers and was important to every logging camp, as he would make tools, fix them if they were broken and sharpen tools so they would be ready to be used by the lumbermen. Perhaps the longest-

The men preparing to break up a log jam just below Orin Falls on the Wassataquoik Stream. *Myron Avery Collection, Maine State Library.*

used and most important early tool was the axe. There are a number of different types of axes, all weighing about four pounds with a three-foot-long handle, but all have the same main parts. Besides the handle, which was made to the preference of the cutter, the important part of the axe is the cutting edge, the first part to come into contact with the wood, and the bevel face, which follows and spreads the wood that is being cut out to be removed. The Maine axe is a single-bladed wedge-type axe with a three-foot handle and a blunt head. The double-bitted axe often seen wielded by Paul Bunyan was invented around the time of the Civil War, but it wasn't until around 1900 that the first double-bitted axe, called the Wisconsin axe or Michigan axe, was used in Maine by a man named William Mann. In the day of tall timber cutting, there were eighteen manufacturers producing axes in the Waterville area alone. At one time, Maine had more than three hundred axe makers to supply the men in the woods. More recently, almost all of the axes sold in Maine are from China. Finally, the last big manufacture of axes, the Snow & Nealley Company, would eventually outsource to China. The Snow & Nealley Company had been making axes in Maine since 1864. However, the company was recently purchased in 2007 by an Amish family from Smyrna and is once again producing axes made in the United States.[131]

While the axe was important, there was another tool that came into play for cutting trees down: the crosscut saw. First used for Pennsylvania logging around 1880, it did not come into play in the Maine woods until around 1900. It was patented in 1861 by a man named Jerome Dietrich. The crosscut saw, or felling saw, is a saw used to cut trees by cutting the wood perpendicular to the grain of the wood in the tree. The design of the saw is such that it is extremely light and flexible, allowing the saw to be pulled, not pushed; the light weight does not allow gravity to hold the blade against the tree, causing it to jam or get stuck. The blade is curved so that the cutters can place a wedge into the cut to prevent it from further jamming the saw. The saw had two types of teeth: the first are the cutting teeth, used to cut the wood; the second is called a raker tooth, used to remove the cut wood so that there is a clean surface for the cutter teeth. These teeth alternate along the length of the saw. The crosscut saw blade and the chainsaw blade are both designed using the same types of teeth. Today, skilled men with a crosscut saw can cut wood just as fast as a skilled man with chainsaw, which has been shown time and time again in logging competitions.

Once the tree was cut down, it had to be moved, which is where the next tool comes into play. Most men cutting and moving timber carried a tool called a peavey. In 1858, a blacksmith named Joseph Peavey of Stillwater, Maine, was given credit for the invention. The peavey that is used today was an 1873 modification of the original peavey made by his grandson, James Henry Peavey, that had a solid socket with a pick attached, soon to be called the rafting peavey, which is the same tool that is used today by many workers in the woods. The peavey is a refinement of a tool called the cant dog, which was a tool used in sawmills to turn timber for re-sawing. It was a shaft with a hook on the end used to move the timber to be cut. Joseph Peavey added a point to the bottom, giving it added versatility. It could be used to roll logs, break log jams, pry rocks, tighten chains and roll trees that did not fall to the ground when cut, or it could be used for just about anything the logger could not do by hand once the tree was cut. The peavey is typically about five feet long with a four-inch spike protruding from the bottom and a hook a short distance up the shaft; they can also reach up to eight or nine feet in length. The spike is rammed into a log, and then the pivot arm hook grabs the log at a second location. Once the log is connected to the peavey, the person using the peavey has tremendous leverage to move the log by rolling it. The peavey, as well as other tools used in the timber industry, is still manufactured by the Peavey Manufacturing Company in Eddington, Maine.[132]

Once the logs were in the water and moving, the river driver used a pike pole, the same type of tool that was used as a weapon in medieval times. It was a long pole with a twisted pointed metal end used for reaching, holding, pushing and pulling logs floating down the river. The metal end came in two types: one with a point and hook in one end for pushing or pulling logs and the other (more commonly used on flat water) a metal point with a twist, used to hold a log in place but which could be easily and quickly removed by the river driver. The quick twist of the pole would allow the river driver to remove the point from a log. The pike pole was also used for balance when the men were standing on the moving logs going down the stream.

The men's boots—leather nail-soled boots known as caulks,[133] sometimes called hobnailed boots—were uniquely designed for the river drivers. The nails in the bottom gave them traction on the floating logs and were a life saver for those men riding the logs downstream. The men were very protective of their boots, often carrying them tied together over their shoulder to protect the spikes[134] when they were not on the river. To give an idea of how important these boots were to the river driver, when a river driver would die from an accident on the river, his companions would often bury him along the side of the stream and hang his boots off a tree nearby. You can often find the soles of these boots around the old logging camps. The boots are still in use today

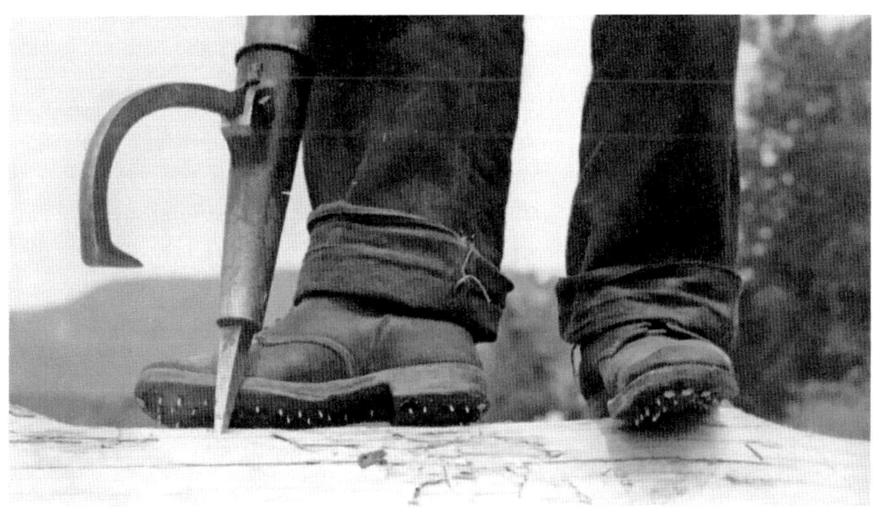

Close-up view of two important items used by the loggers. On the left is a peavey, and on the right are caulks or hobnailed boots. *Millinocket Historical Society.*

by loggers in many places but are no longer protected the way they were in the past; today, they are just for traction on wet timber in the forest.

On the river, the straighter the flow of logs the faster they would move downstream, so a number of different booms were used. There are two types of booms: the side boom was a string of logs anchored on both ends, designed to keep the floating logs in the river and not go up small streams or into a swamp; the other type was called a shear boom, used to keep the logs in the main flow of the stream. The upriver end was anchored, while the downstream end floated free; a wing was constructed using a second log, creating an "A" shape and holding the logs in the flow of the river. The boom itself was constructed of long logs, generally about twenty feet long with a two-inch hole drilled in both ends. A chain with a metal ring in one end was placed in the hole at one end, while at the other end of the chain there was a pivoting "T" section that was placed through the hole in another log until the boom was the correct length. Some of the longer floating booms were more than 1 mile in length.[135]

When the logs finally entered the main river, another tool would come into play. The bateau, or river boat, would come onto the drive. The drivers would often arrive and leave the worksite by way of this boat, a European watercraft that was used during most of the early wars in the United States; you often see paintings of George Washington crossing the Delaware River in one. The bateau was light, nimble and able to take tremendous punishment. The standard Maine river bateau was thirty-two feet long and four feet deep, with a flat bottom measuring twenty-two feet long by three feet wide. This allowed the boat to have great buoyancy and stability, while at the same time the small wetted surface allowed greater maneuverability and the ability to pole the bateau around the moving water easily. The bateau generally weighed between eight and nine hundred pounds but could be carried by a dozen men, including all of their equipment. A man named Hosea Maynard from Bangor was the master bateau builder and constructed most of the bateaux used on the Penobscot in the early years, producing seventy-five or more each year. The bateau was used to transport the river drivers as well as the cook both downriver and upriver, transport supplies to the riverside camps and in general keep a careful eye on the drive's progress.[136]

With the tools in hand, the river drivers were ready to move the timber downstream, but first they had to get the timber to the water's edge. The land baron's surveyor would lay out the location for the storage of the timber, roads to be used and the twitch trails (small side roads) for the cutters. Once the timber was cut, all branches removed and logs sized

The Deasey Dam booming ground was a place where the logs were collected so that they could be moved downstream in a group. *Patten Lumbermen's Museum.*

and marked, the timber was moved to what was called a log yard. The log yard was a location where the logs were piled, sorted for value and the marks checked before they took their trip to the river's edge and then on to the market. Log yards are still used today and can be found on almost all active logging roads; as you drive by, you will see various-size logs in different piles based on species and grade. Getting the wood to the log yards required the use of teams of workhorses. These animals were well cared for and able to pull huge piles of wood to the log yards using the twitch trails laid out by the surveyor; when the terrain was extremely steep or rough, the logs were hauled by oxen. Once in a central location, the logs were moved to the riverside using narrow iced roads. The winter roads were banked on both sides by either dirt or logs, and then water was added to ice the roads, allowing the sleds to be pulled more easily. Oftentimes the horse teams were so good that in flat terrain they did not even need a driver. The animals would bring the logs to where they were to be stored, and once the logs were unloaded, they would return to the cutting location. The operation of pulling cut timber out of a forest is called "skidding," in which the logs are transported from the cutting site to log yard by being dragged along the ground. The process is still the same today, but a heavy vehicle with large chained tires called a skidder does the work.

In 1901, a new piece of machinery showed up in the Maine woods: the Lombard hauler. A Waterville blacksmith named Alvin Lombard patented the first continuous track vehicle propulsion system for commercial use on May 21, 1901. The log hauler requires a team of four men to operate: the engineer and fireman occupied the cab in the back of the engine, where they controlled the speed and fed the boiler; up front was the steersman as he sat in front of the engine to steer the machine; and the conductor rode on the sleds to keep an eye on the load and signal the crew in the cab with a rope bell. In 1914, Lombard began to make six-cylinder gasoline-powered log haulers. He even tried to build a diesel engine, but the internal combustion log hauler, which was called Lombard tractor, was much less powerful than the steam model. While the steam Lombard hauler, which looked like a twenty-ton snowmobile, could only go five miles per hour and cost $5,000,[137] it could haul as much as three hundred tons of timber or as much as 1 million board feet of timber; it often created its own roads as it moved through the forest. The system that Lombard developed was later used for military tanks during World War I and today is still being used for tractors and construction equipment. The steam hauler was used until 1929, and by the close of World War I, the loggers were making a slow transition from horses and haulers to bulldozers and tractors to move the timber.

In the early years, the logs were taken to the yard or the edge of streams by horses or oxen, but difficult terrain changed the techniques that had to be developed to allow them to make the trip with the largest load possible. One method was called carding, where the logs were moved down very small streams suspended on logs that were placed at forty-five-degree angles to the sides of the stream. The logs crossing the stream were placed such that when one reached the other edge, a new log would be started on that same edge in a zig-zag pattern all the way down the stream. The logs to be removed would then be pulled over the logs that crossed the stream until they reached the edge of the river, where they would be able to float. If the terrain was steep, they would often use a snub line to slow the load going downhill—a steel cable would be attached to the back of the sled and then wrapped around a tree for friction. One of the men would let the steel cable out slowly as the sled moved down the hill; often the snub tree would catch fire due to the friction on the steel cable. Another method used in several locations involved wooden flumes where the logs could be run down a flume constructed of rough timber. Sometimes the flumes were small, allowing logs to pass one at a time, but often the whole river would be lined with logs to direct their flow where the drivers wanted it to go.

While there were some logs that were lost during the drive, most would make it to market, which is where new problems would begin. All of the companies used the same river, so there needed to be some way to separate the logs belonging to each company. In the log yard, the scaler or surveyor would mark the end of each log for grade and ownership. An honest scaler was an asset to the company, as he would be the only person who knew how much wood was being cut. Some scalers even used what was called a bucking board in the camp kitchen or sleeping area as an incentive to the lumbermen. Each night, he would post on the door the amount of wood cut and hauled by each teamster; while they were not paid more for cutting the most, it became a matter of pride to be the best. The scaler used an axe with a brand in the end to stamp each log so that they could be separated by ownership at the mill based on where the logs were cut and by whom. This method is still used today, often marking the ends of the logs for grade and ownership with either paint or a lumber crayon.

Once the timber was cut and scaled, they had to move it to market down the river or across watersheds. The lumbermen of the day used

Riverside landing where the logs were prepared for the river drive. Notice that all the logs have a brand to show ownership at the market. *Patten Lumbermen's Museum.*

many different methods of moving long logs to market. They dug canals, built sluiceways, constructed dams and even built railways in the wilderness. The object was to get the timber to market as cheaply as possible, and that meant using the flow of the water to help move the timber downstream. The higher the lumbermen moved into the mountains, the more innovative they would have to become to get the timber out. They realized that the streams and rivers had to be controlled in order to use them successfully. The early river drives depended on the spring freshet,[138] which would vary from year to year depending on the snowpack and spring rains. Many of the river drives would become hung (jammed and stuck) as the water started to dry up, which would mean that no logs would make it to market and there would be no return on the owner's investment.

The lumbermen were primarily in the business of transporting logs from the stump to the stream and then delivering them to the boom at the market. At the edge of the stream, the logs would be piled in a landing, but first the banks were prepared by lining them with thirty-foot logs perpendicular to the stream, spaced out every ten feet. Then the logs to be driven were placed on these roller logs in tiers back up the bank of the river, sometimes as high as a three-story building. When the water was at the correct level, the men would break the rollaway log, and the pile would roll into the water. Generally, it would take four or five men to break the tiers, which was an extremely dangerous task in an already dangerous business. The men would have to remove the key log and then get out of the way before the pile crashed down on top of them.

The early river drivers were at the mercy of the melting snow, but in the high country, the snow was sometimes either slow to melt or melted too quickly. The early drive was often hung, as the water became too low to float the logs. At other times, the water would be so high that the logs moved in an uncontrollable manner down the stream and into the forest at the edge of the water. The first loggers in the Wassataquoik Valley gave up, leaving behind piles of pine logs thirty feet high in places just to rot because they could not get them out. The lumbermen realized that they had to control the spring flow of the stream if they wanted to maximize the drive. The lumbermen built all types of crib dams to control the flow and direct the drive. All of the crib dams used the same basic construction method. Crib dams were nothing more than a pyramid of poles or lumber laid crisscross at regular intervals and then filled in with rocks and gravel. Some of the dams would have gates to

A group of men loading long logs onto a sled for the horses to pull to the landing near the river. *Patten Lumbermen's Museum.*

control the flow, while others were simply constructed to increase the velocity and direction of the flow of the stream. Using this method, the lumbermen built more than two dozen crib dams on the Wassataquoik Stream alone to control the spring flow. The dams were often washed out by summer storms or a quick release of water in the spring but would be rebuilt each year. As the removal of the timber moved from the valleys to the mountaintops, the lumbermen would construct various sluices for the logs; canals were even constructed to move the logs across watersheds. There was really nothing that they would not do to get the logs out of the forest to market.[139]

Once the logs were in the water and the flow was made somewhat constant by the dams, the real work of the river drive began. As the logs moved downriver, they would fetch-up on rocks. Once one was caught, generally more would follow until they had a log-jammed stream to untangle. The river drivers would work in groups to unjam the logs. To prevent these types of jams, the river drivers would build a wooden sluice or rock-walled sections called wing dams or just blow the rocks up using

A group of men picking the rear of the drive; most of the work was making sure that every log made it downstream to the boom. *Myron Avery Collection, Maine State Library.*

dynamite. To break up a jam, the river drivers would work to uncover the key log or center of the jam. Once the correct log or logs were moved, the drive would continue down the stream. This had to be done quickly because the water would be backing up behind the jam and the pressure would increase. If the jam broke unexpectedly, the river driver had to move quickly to get out of the way. Some small jams along the edge were left in place as wing dams to keep the logs floating in the center of the stream. Once the logs were well on their way downstream, about 80 percent of the crew would follow the drive, going down the stream cleaning up or picking the rear logs along the edge. The primary tool used for this work was a peavey. At the end of the drive, the men were paid, but first their room, board and other expenses had to be deducted, often leaving them with little money to take home to their families. They would head home to their families until the fall, when timber cutting would begin again. Some men never made it out of the forest, killed in an explosion, drowned in a log jam or crushed by a falling tree—it was dangerous work.

More than 80 percent of the drive was picking the rear. Here in a small stream, the four-foot pulp is being added to the stream flow. *Millinocket Historical Society.*

The river drive on the Wassataquoik Stream ended in 1919 due to fires and floods, while the drives ended on the Penobscot with Great Northern Paper Company after the 1971 drive. The last log drive in America was on the Kennebec River in western Maine in the spring and summer of 1976.[140] River log driving came to an end as a result of the federal Clean Water Act of 1972, ushered into law by Maine's Senator Edmund Muskie, and a Maine law that banned log driving after October 31, 1976. A great many logs never made it to market over the years, sinking to the bottom, where they remained in an environment that did not allow them to rot. Today, the rivers drives are gone, and the forest roads have been carved all over the Maine woods for trucks and machinery to do the work that streams, rivers and men had done for two hundred years. But the end of the river drives and those logs that have sat at the bottom of the Maine's lakes and rivers have given birth to a new business. The heritage timber industry removes those logs from the bottom of the lakes, improving the environment while at the same time creating a new market. What makes heritage timber important is that these are 100 percent reclaimed logs, many of which were at one time virgin timber. The wood is high-end timber, rich in color, character and a beautiful large, straight grain that is full of history. The wood has not been exposed to modern-day chemicals and can be made into everything from flooring to cabinets. It is a great way to improve the environment while at the same time having a bit of Maine's logging history in your home.

CHAPTER 8

UPPER RIVER SPORTING CAMPS

When it comes to camps on the upper East Branch of the Penobscot River, we are looking at the area just below the Grand Falls, a section that starts near the mouth of Bowlin Stream and continues several miles downstream. In the early years, this area was accessed using the American Thread Road out of Patten. With the American Thread Road almost reaching the river, it was not long before lumbermen turned to recreational guests, guiding and other woods activities to make a living. The first to arrive was Charles E. McDonald from Sherman, who in 1895 opened his camps just downstream from the mouth of Bowlin Brook. The camps at the time were called the Bowlan Camps; it is difficult to understand the reason for the different spellings that were used in various advertisements.

The McDonald Camps, as they were known in the early years, had yearly advertisements in the Bangor & Aroostook Railroad magazine *In the Maine Woods*, encouraging visitors to not only use the camps but also travel using B&A trains. The camp in the beginning had only one building, still standing and used today: the small one-room cabin that sits in the center of the current facility is in operation today as a sleeping cabin. But soon Bowlin Camps had a main dining room and lounging camps, as well as a number of smaller sleeping cabins. Charles McDonald boasted of having a large string of outlying camps covering a huge territory that had more than fifteen ponds and brooks for the sportsmen. He had eight outpost camps that were located at many of the local ponds. On the east side of the river, he had camps located at Kimball Pond and Bowlin Ponds to the northeast and

Above: A steam Lombard hauler owned by the Merrill Lumber Company, which opened the area to recreational use with its constructed logging roads. *Patten Lumbermen's Museum.*

Opposite: Bowlin Camp ads used in the railroad's sporting guide. They encouraged people to use the train to gain access to the wilderness. *From* In the Maine Woods, *B&A, 1905.*

Lunksoos Pond to the southeast. On the west side of the river, he had camps located at McDonald Pond and Messer Pond, two camps near Traveler Pond and one on the ridge above Hathorn Pond. He offered all the comforts of home in the deep wilderness for his visitors. His camps were considered to be moderately priced considering the location and what they had to offer the fisherman or hunter. They were not accessible by automobile, but he was able to bring sports in by packhorse or buckboard the nine miles from Patten. Guests could also travel by motor canoe from downstream, leaving from the Grindstone railroad station.[141]

One of his accomplishments was a trip that he developed where the guests would be taken to South Branch Pond by saddle and packhorse. It was a long trip, but it was advertised as climbing to 2,900 feet to offer exceptional views of the surrounding areas. He had two mountain camps that he had constructed for his guests to stay in during their trip. The horses and guide would take the guests across the river at the mouth of Bowlin Brook and then downstream through a rock-lined cut in the ridges that is still

In the Wild Heart of Maine

For those who love the wild there exists no more attractive place than the **Bowlan Camps** on the East Branch of the Penobscot River. Here awaits a wealth of ideal trout fishing and excellent big game shooting. The camp, located on the river bank, is in the midst of fifteen ponds and as many brooks, all stocked with native trout, connected by trails and provided with permanent camps for casual visitors or for those who desire to be alone. Trout are rising all summer—and such trout! Summer visitors are assured of the most comfortable quarters, the best country table, and the wildest, most impressive scenery in all Maine.

BOWLAN CAMPS

A card will bring an illustrated booklet. When you tire of the trout fishing there are canoeing, the mountains for climbing, and a string of excellent saddle horses for your convenience. Lounging camp with large stone fireplace. Separate sleeping camps.

In the fall the shooting is of the best. Bear, Moose and Deer abound.

CHARLIE McDONALD, - Sherman, Maine

Typical use of packhorses to carry gear and people to the various outpost camps. People could make longer trips that were always guided. *Bert Call Collection, Special Collections, Raymond H. Fogler Library.*

there today. They would then travel just to the south of Messer Pond, where there was a camp if needed. Then it was on up to Traveler Pond, where they would stay before continuing up to Traveler Gap and either climbing Traveler Mountain or going down to the South Branch Ponds.

Several miles downstream, there was a fish hatchery used to support the Atlantic salmon fishery in the Penobscot River. A man named Charles Atkins played a pivotal role in the Atlantic salmon hatchery on the river located at the month of Little Spring Brook, across the river from Sufferers Rock, which is a ledge outcrop about fourteen miles downstream from the Grand Lake Dam.[142] Charles Atkins and Nathan Foster were the first Maine Fisheries commissioners, and in their first report on January 1868, they stated that "the salmon is suffering from neglect and persecution."[143] Congress followed the states' lead, creating the U.S. Commission on Fish and Fisheries on February 9, 1871, the forerunner of the U.S. Fish and Wildlife Service. Spencer Baird was appointed its first commissioner, and among his first directives were to conduct studies on the decline of coastal and inland food fishes and methods of fish culture. Baird turned to Charles Atkins for his expertise and directed him to locate a suitable sites in Maine to raise Atlantic salmon.

In 1871, Atkins opened the Craig Brook Hatchery. Atlantic salmon eggs were taken only from the Penobscot River beginning in 1871, as well as from 1871 to 1875 and from 1879 to 1919. Besides the hatchery at Craig Brook, the federal government opened hatcheries at Bucksport in 1872, Sebec Lake in 1873, Grand Lake Stream in 1875, Green Lake in Dedham in 1892, Upper Penobscot in 1903 and the Salem Feeding Station in 1941.[144] Atkins opened the Upper Penobscot Auxiliary Station (Little Spring Brook Hatchery) in the fall of 1903, and it operated until the spring of 1916.[145] It operated each year from October or November through May or June. Eyed eggs from Craig Brook were taken by train to Stacyville and then by wagon to the Little Spring Brook facility. After yolk sacs were absorbed, in May and June, all of the fry were released into the East Branch. Because the facility did not have the ability to produce food or feed the fish, they were released as soon as the egg sac was gone. The vast majority of salmon stocked in the Penobscot drainage each year from 1904 to 1916 were produced at the Little Spring Brook facility. The facility was closed in 1916 for unknown reasons—it may have been weather, floods, fire or disease, but we will never know for sure. After 1919, things went downhill quickly. Penobscot salmon runs and the fishery continued to decline in the 1920s and '30s until it was almost nonexistent.[146] Today, efforts have been renewed and continue to work toward restoring a self-sustaining population of sea-run Atlantic salmon.

At this same location, there were a number of historical camps on both sides of the river. In 1901, a sporting camp was established at the mouth of Little Spring Brook by Ed Whitehouse of Sherman and Frank C. Cram of Stacyville; the location was known for exceptional salmon fishing.[147] The camp was constructed on the bluff overlooking the river just downstream from the mouth of the stream. Once the hatchery was constructed, Charles McDonald built an outpost camp across the river near what is called Sufferers Rock. The 1908 Sufferers Rock aluminum marker is on the ledge outcrop that sticks out into the river. The marker was used to determine where dams could be constructed on the river for power or storage.

The camps on the west side of the river were taken over in the early 1920s by William F. Tracy and Prince A. Tracy of Stacyville. Their home was located at the beginning of the Stacyville Tote Road in Stacyville (the entrance to the Swift Brook Road), leading into the Hunt Farm. The

Shin Pond House was a first-class hotel used by people seeking adventure in the wilderness. *Bert Call Collection, Special Collections, Raymond H. Fogler Library.*

camps became known as Tracy's Camps. They had a number of outpost camps where guests could go for exceptional fishing or hunting. William Tracy's best-known remote camp, called the Hathorn Camps, was located at Hathorn Pond, and in 1935, William would guide guests to the camp for three dollars per night. With Charles McDonald pushing deeper into the wilderness with his horse trips, William Tracy did the same and established camps at the remote Russell Pond. He cut a trail from his camps on the East Branch of the Penobscot River over the mountains to the mouth of Robar Brook on the Wassataquoik Stream. From there, he followed the Wassataquoik Tote Road deep into the heart of the watershed to Russell Pond. His camps were so successful that in 1943 he was offered the job as patrol ranger for the Russell Pond area of Baxter State Park, where he would use his skills and horses for fire patrol.

Another camp was a bit farther downstream and was known as Bark Camp Meadow, located just to the north of the Monument Line on the west bank of the East Branch of the Penobscot River.[148] While this was not a traditional sporting camp, it was extremely important to the leather industry. It was the collection location for hemlock bark. The eastern hemlock played a crucial role in the early hide-tanning industry. Some of the larger local tanneries would use twelve thousand cords of bark annually in the process of tanning hides; the tanneries had to be located close to the source of the bark. The tanneries would pay six dollars per cord delivered in 1895.[149] Early harvesters obtained hemlock bark by cutting down the tree and then peeling the bark off as far as was practicable, cutting it into four-foot strips. The tree's trunk was left to rot in the forest, as the bark was the only desired product. This location was on the northern edge of the hemlock range. At one time, Island Falls and Winn had the largest and northernmost of all the tanneries in North America; there was also a large tannery location on the river in Medway.[150]

The hemlock bark collecting took place from May to August because that was when the trees were growing very rapidly, creating new wood that was soft and slippery under the bark. The crew generally consisted of four men: a chopper, a knotter, a ringer and splitter/spudder. Using an axe, the ringer would cut around the base and then again four feet up the tree; then he would split the bark up the length of the cut. Next would come the spudder, who had the job of removing the bark. The spud is a chisel-like tool with a curved blade at the end and sharpened on three sides to fit the shape of the log; this was forced into the split, removing the bark from the tree. Then the chopper would cut the tree down, with the knotter removing the branches; then the ringer would go back to work. They always worked from the bottom of the tree to the top.

The bark was placed in small piles near the felled tree and collected into larger piles along roads for loading on sleds to be hauled to the tanneries in the early winter. At the tannery, which was conveniently sited on the river, the bark was ground or shredded and placed in a series of tubs filled with hot water. Using a passive method, it took about four days for the tannins to leach out of the bark—steam infusions halved the time, with the old bark being dried and used for fuel to heat the vats. The resulting tanning liquor was then circulated through the tanning vats in increasingly acidic solutions. The use of hemlock bark was made obsolete by the development of chemical processes for tanning hides, and these riverside tanneries quickly disappeared, as did the process of collecting bark.

The bark from this location fed two tannery locations in the area. In Island Falls, located on the West Branch of the Mattawamkeag River, was the mill owned by Franks W. Hunt & Sons, operating out of Boston. The bark would have been delivered using the American Thread Road. This mill, built in 1818, was the largest sole leather tannery to be built in the state of Maine, as well as the last using the bark process to close in Maine. The Maine State

The spud is a chisel-like tool with a curved blade at the end and sharpened on three sides to fit the shape of the log; it was forced into the split, removing the bark from the tree. *Millinocket Historical Society.*

Register shows the mill still operating in 1920 before closing for good. But in the case of hemlock bark from Bark Camp Meadow, more than likely it would have been moved downriver to the mill in Medway. This tannery was constructed in 1870 by Henry Poor & Son, consuming a bit more than ten thousand cords of bark each year.[151]

The trees that remained behind in the cold, damp, acidic forest would just sit on the ground, covered by leaves, never rotting. While Bark Camp Meadow still remains, the only evidence of this once important industry are some artifacts and the mounds of bark and logs left in the woods from long ago. It is tannin, not pollution, that gives many of the Northeast streams and brooks their root beer brown color.

The state also worked to improve the fisheries in the area, with a historical fish hatchery on the Owlsboro Road in Mount Chase, but in reality, this served as a trout rearing station or feeding station. Willis Parson, Maine commissioner of inland fisheries and game, had the station constructed using funds appropriated by the 1923 legislature. The station was needed because there was no nearby hatchery from which brook trout could be distributed to the numerous ponds in the vicinity for sportsmen. The land for the station was donated by concerned local citizens and sporting camp owners. The station was simply a series of pools fed by a small, nearby dammed cold-water stream that flowed into Peavey Brook. It consisted of a canal that formed seven rearing pools, supplied by the cold water from the brook. The fingerlings were hatched at the Enfield hatchery to the south and shipped to Patten by railroad, arriving at night and taken to the feeding station to be distributed at a later date in the area. It would be interesting to know how far the trout from the feeding station were placed—was it just at the very local ponds such as Shin Pond and Rockabema Lake, or were they taken farther into Baxter State Park or the Katahdin Woods and Waters National Monument to stock those more remote ponds?[152]

Today, Bowlin Camps are still operating, with one of its original camps still being used. The camps are accessible by automobile and still used for a

While most of the old camps have returned to the wilderness, Bowlin Camp, constructed in 1895, still has one of its original cabins. *Bowlin Camps Photograph.*

wide range of recreational activities. Sufferers Rock and the survey marker are still located on a ledge outcrop across from Little Spring Brook. The trail to Traveler Gap is now overgrown, as is the Tracy Trail to Robar Brook. All of the outlying camps are long gone. The camps around the mouth of Little Spring Brook have only a bit of cement and metal serving as reminders of their past glory.

CHAPTER 9

WILDERNESS WILDFIRES

Logging in the early days was difficult, but Mother Nature made life even harder for the lumbermen as they moved into the wilderness in search of timber. It would be impossible to look at the logging history of the area without taking the time to looking at the role Mother Nature played in shaping the area's forest. One of the reasons that Katahdin Woods and Waters National Monument is such a special place is due to the damage done by wildfire more than one hundred years ago. The wildfires were so hot that much of the organic material in the forests west of the East Branch of the Penobscot River was completely destroyed, causing an extremely slow period of revegetation. This slow regrowth of the forest has given way to a much more diverse forest community. Within the monument, there have been more than twenty-four different plant communities identified by ecologists. Each of these plant communities supports its own species of birds and animals. There were four major wildfires, all started by humans, that have played an important role in shaping today's living landscape, and we will look at these wildfires within the monument, as well as take a look at forest protection in the monument.

The 1825 Miramichi Fire was one of the largest mega-wildfires ever recorded in North America. In 1815, the British empire had a need for timber, something that New Brunswick could produce using indentured laborers, mostly Scots and Irish. They started to cut along the New Brunswick coast, the laborers coming from a land where less than 2 percent was forest covered; they mostly recognized fire as a way of clearing fields to grow crops.

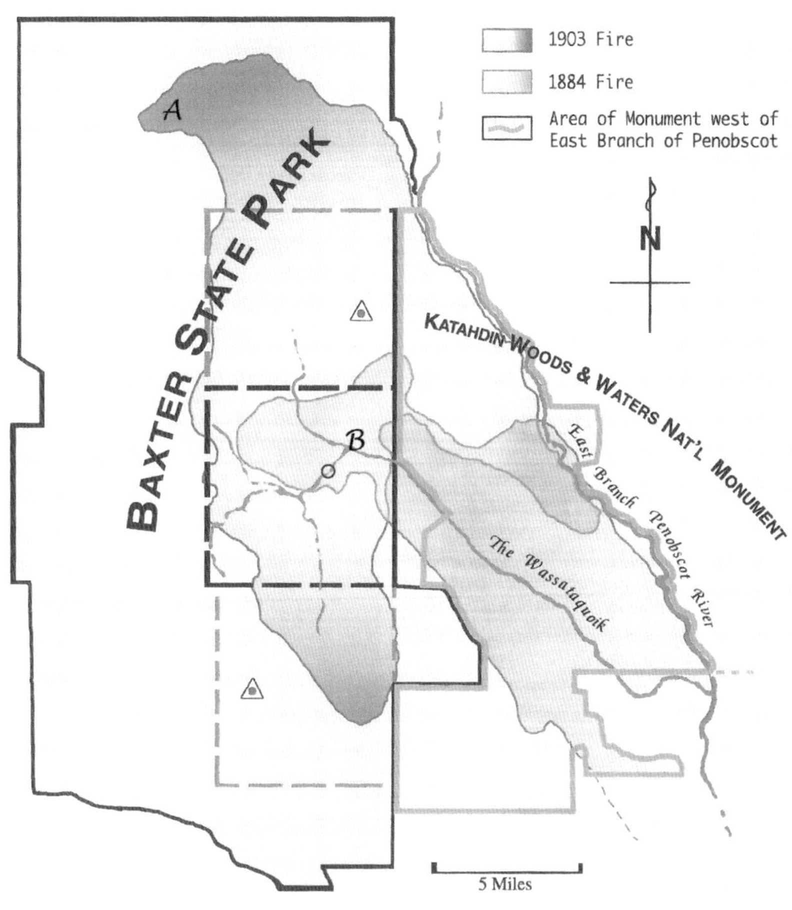

This map by Dr. Gary Boone shows the starting location and burned area for the 1903 (A) and the 1884 (B) wildfires, with their relationships to the monument.

So, on October 7, 1825, when the fire started, the workers just ignored it. But as night closed and gale-force winds started to blow, before long the fire traveled up the Miramichi River west into Maine, burning everything in its path.[153] By the time the fire was finally extinguished, several hundred people had been killed and thousands had been left homeless. The area of the fire was estimated to be 5 million acres of forested land, which included almost 1 million acres in northeastern Maine[154]—an area larger than the size of the state of Rhode Island was burned within northern Maine. At the time, it was the greatest wildfire of North American's record history; it was even used in 1861 as an example when Horace Greeley debated Henry David Thoreau on the theory of forests' spontaneous regeneration after wildfire.[155] All that stopped the fire was the sudden extremely rainy weather, the East Branch of the Penobscot River and the mountains around Katahdin. Even the great explorer Myron Keep noticed the results of the fire during his climbs up the mountain in later years. The fire had the greatest intensity around Miramichi, with the outer area mostly burning quickly across the tree tops, which is called a crown fire.

The next wildfire was known as the Great State Bonfire of 1826. It was a period of time when the State of Maine owned all the northern timber. Timber theft was a major problem, as loggers would go in during the fall to cut hay for their oxen and then cut the timber in the winter to be moved by water in the spring. According to folklore, Jim Chase, a woods-wise surveyor, was hired by the state to stop the thievery. One hot August day, he went into the woods and set the hay on fire so the thieves would have nothing to feed their oxen. As he burned the stacks of hay, the wind picked up and set the forest on fire. The fire burned for two weeks before heavy rain finally put it out, allowing Jim Chase to return from the forest. When all was said and done, the fire had burned five entire townships and parts of six other townships for a total of more than two hundred square miles of the finest timber the state had to offer. The value of what was burned was far greater than what would have been stolen by the thieves.[156]

The first recorded regional wildfire was in 1837,[157] but the extent of the fire is unknown other than that it was an extensive burning of timber east down the Wassataquoik Valley. Much of the evidence of this forest fire was obliterated by latter forest fires in the area. But all remaining evidence points to the final edge of the forest fire being located in the area of where Deasey Dam would later be built. Then in the fall of 1883 came the start of what would destroy the Wassataquoik Valley completely for the first time. On November 12, 1883, there was a late fall hurricane known as the "Maine Cyclone" that blew down most of the timber on the southwest side of Deasey Mountain. So much timber blew down that it became stacked, with much of it never touching the ground, leaving loggers with a winter plan to cut the wind-thrown timber in the 1883–84 cutting season.

On June 29, 1884, some fisherman on the Wassataquoik Stream near Norway Falls built a large campfire to drive away mosquitoes. The fire quickly got out of control, as it had been extremely dry that spring, and the loggers had left slash from the winter operation everywhere. The wind

Looking at the aftermath of the 1884 wildfire on the ridge above Orin Falls. *Lucius Merrill Collection, Bangor Public Library.*

was calm, so the fire spread slowly in all directions, burning everything off the ground. But the next day, on June 30, the wind started to pick up. By midday, it would have been considered an extremely strong wind that was able to push the fire downstream and to the northeast. It burned to the base of Traveler Mountain and south to the top of Lunksoos Mountain and the Wassataquoik Range and then eastward toward the East Branch of the Penobscot River. Although it was unable to cross the river, there were no other efforts to control the fire; it was only stopped by heavy rains on July 3, left to smolder. Twenty-two thousand acres of forestland burned, including most of the lumber camps and dams built by the Tracy and Love operation.

Tracy and Love were quick to rebuild their camps, cutting as much of the fallen charred timber as they could before it was no longer useful. The forest was littered with suspended trees that refused to rot; they just became drier and drier until June 2, 1903, when another great wildfire burned for less than a week, claiming 276,587 acres or 132 square miles of forest.[158] In the summer of 1903, Maine had 355 wildfires, with many small fires put out by community fire wardens. The spring of 1903 was the driest season on record, with the largest spring rainfall on April 25 amounting to only 0.46 inches of rain. The origin of the wildfire is believed to have been a gang of men who were constructing a telephone line near Webster Lake. It was standard practice for the workers to smoke pipes while they worked, and once they were finished, they would empty the bowl of ashes onto the ground, not realizing that it often still contained hot embers.

It would be a full day after the wildfire started, on Wednesday June 3, 1903, that it would grow with the strong winds blowing hard from the northwest, driving the fire south. By the time the fire reached Trout Brook to the south, it was totally out of control. The three necessary conditions favoring a wildfire all came together that day: plenty of fuel in the way of dry dead trees and slash, heavy winds blowing in the direction of the fuel and no natural barriers to stop the fire. The wildfire raced through Pogy Notch between the mountains and into the Wassataquoik Valley, burning everything in its path. The southern movement of the wildfire was stopped and turned by Turner Mountain, and the east-moving wildfire was stopped by the waters of the East Branch of the Penobscot River. It is unknown when the wildfire was completely over, but it had lost most of its blaze by Friday, June 5, and the extremely heavy rain of Tuesday, June 9, extinguished it completely. Once the wildfire was over, there were a number of small spots not burned by either the 1884 or 1903 fires, most notably the east face of Lunksoos Mountain (steep rocky terrain), and a 25-acre plot on the Wassataquoik Tote Road near where it crosses the town line, a very swampy area. Otherwise, it completely burned more than 84,480 acres of forest in just three days.[159] It burned so quickly that today there are still large remains of charred trees standing throughout the area to the west of the river.[160]

Logging returned in 1910, but long logs were no longer the focus; rather, four-foot pulp was being driven down the river. With all of the trees burned and heavy-snow winters followed by a quick snowmelt, spring flooding became a problem. In 1912, the flood and early ice jams washed away the halfway camps, followed by a small upper valley wildfire in 1915. But the final blow to logging on the Wassataquoik came in 1919, when the flash spring flood washed out most of the dams along the stream, bringing all logging to an end. Due in part to the extreme wildfires in the valley, a wide variety of plant communities exists today, making the monument such a special place.

After the catastrophic wildfire season of 1903, the attention shifted to fire detection, with Maine having one of the first fire lookouts in the nation in 1905. In 1918, John E. Mitchell, chief warden of the Upper East Branch

Then the timber was cut, the slash was left on the ground to dry, which caused wildfires to move quickly. *Patten Lumbermen's Museum.*

Waters, and Thomas Griffin, chief warden of Lower Lakes and West Branch Waters, surveyed Lunksoos Mountain as a possible site for a fire lookout to protect the areas to the east of Mount Katahdin. They recommended a lookout there on the bald summit, but it was never built.

The first area lookout was built on Hunt Mountain in 1924, a forty-eight-foot steel tower lookout with an eight-foot-square cabin. Hunt Mountain was selected as the location in part due to the existing crossing at the Hunt Farm on the river. The trail to the lookout crossed the East Branch of the Penobscot River just upstream from the farm using the ford. The trail then headed toward Hunt Mountain up the northeast ridge to the summit. Due to the large expanse of wilderness forest between Hunt Mountain and Mount Katahdin, the tower was a welcome addition, but its location left a large blind spot to the north, where Deasey Mountain blocked the view. So, in 1929, a new lookout was constructed at the bald summit of Deasey Mountain, giving a 360-degree view of the surrounding forest.

The Deasey Mountain Lookout (also known as Daicey Mountain on the fire lookout map) was an eight-foot-square groundhouse constructed by the Maine Forest Service to supplement the area served by the Hunt Mountain lookout. Several years later, in 1931, the Hunt Mountain Lookout was removed and re-erected on Lawler Hill in Benedicta.[161] Austin Brown was on duty at the Deasey Mountain Lookout as the watchman in 1950 when a

In 1950, a RCN Hawker Sea Fury crashed, killing the pilot. The only evidence of the crash came from the fire lookout until it was finally discovered eighteen years later. *Michelle Benoit photograph.*

military RCN Hawker Sea Fury plane crashed. He reported that the plane had flown over at very low altitude several times. His observation was the only information about the lost plane. The crash would remain a mystery until two Great Northern Paper Company foresters discovered the wreckage in February 1968 north of Millinocket. The RCN Hawker Sea Fury crashed in the western part of the monument.

Shortly after the plane had been rebuilt in Toronto, it was to be flown to the HMCS *Shearwater* in Dartmouth, Nova Scotia. The plane had been damaged a year earlier, when the main landing gear buckled during an emergency landing in Ontario. On Friday, June 30, 1950, Royal Canadian Navy lieutenant Mervin Hare was assigned as the test pilot, given the task of ferrying the newly overhauled plane from Toronto to Dartmouth. Around noon, the plane took off from Quebec City after a stop and proceeded to put on a brief show of high-speed aerobatics before flying off to the east. The plane's flight plan was to take it across northern Maine and eastern New Brunswick and then on to Nova Scotia. When the plane failed to arrive at its home base, a massive international air search was launched. The problem was that the flight path was over uninhabited forests on both sides of the border, where the plane could have made a forced landing or crashed. After five days, the U.S. search was called off, with no evidence of the crash within a search area that stretched from Katahdin to the Canadian border. Seven days later, the Canadian search was also called off. A later RCN examination of the wreckage located parachute parts and other evidence that the pilot had not bailed out. However, the pilot's remains were never recovered, so a small ridge is the final resting place of the navy lieutenant. The examination of the crash site indicated that the plane came down in a low angle after a high-speed dive, flying almost true north, clipping a tree and leaving a large impact crater.[162]

Another interesting watchman was Ed Werler, who served in 1947. Ed Werler and his wife traveled to the area and fell in love with it. In 1947, he took the watchman's job before becoming the Baxter State Park ranger at Chimney Pond and writing a book about his experience in the Northwoods mountains. The book, *The Call of Katahdin: Life in the Wheeler Woods*, details his experiences as a watchman and then as a ranger.

Over the years, the lookout underwent many changes. In 1955, the Deasey watchman's camp took delivery of a new cookstove, which was moved a distance of 6.25 miles—5 miles by canoe and then 1.25 miles up the mountain on a one-wheel deer carrier with four men, one on each corner. In 1963, the lookout was largely rebuilt, requiring eleven helicopter trips to haul the building materials to the summit. It was officially closed in 1970 but fixed up once again in 1987 by Jim Dyer. It was last used by volunteers for the month of July 1989. The lookout was then re-restored by the International Appalachian Trail organization in 2004 and has been maintained by it. It was nominated for the National Register by Bill Cobb, and on March 15, 2006, it was placed on the National Historic Lookout Register.[163]

At the time, there was no state east of the Mississippi River that offered a better field experience in forestry. Maine was considered to be at the forefront of forest fire protection, and each year, there was a forestry field camp held at Lunksoos Camps on the East Branch of the Penobscot River. Now all that remains of those days of fire is an extremely biologically diverse forest, the groundhouse built in 1929 and the remains of burned trees still standing guard throughout the forest.

CHAPTER 10

SHAPING THE MONUMENT

GEOLOGICAL ACTIVITY

When you think of the shaping of the monument, you have to look at the bedrock below and the glacial shape of the surface above. The rock that gives the general structure to the monument is referred to as the underlying bedrock, and its geology within the monument is dominated in the south by what is called the Katahdin pluton, composed of granite from the Devonian age. The pluton is a granitic mass of molten rock that was buried deep in the earth, allowing it to cool extremely slowly, forming the beautiful rock that give character to much of Maine. It was formed just over 400 million years ago during the early Devonian age.[164] The northern part of the monument is composed of Traveler rhyolite and Matagamon sandstone. The older rocks move to the southeast from Haskell Rock to Grand Pitch. These rocks are in an arch-like structure called an anticline. This feature is called the Weeksboro–Lunksoos Lake anticline, which was worn down by the movement of the glaciers. These rocks have been eroded, with the oldest rocks from the Cambrian age (542 million years ago) found at Grand Pitch, which is the center of the anticline.[165] The Grand Pitch formation has been altered; even the casual observer can see that the rocks have been deformed. These rocks were deformed and folded by the Paleozoic mountain building events long ago.

There were three recognized events that shaped these rocks: the Penobscot event, more than 500 million years ago; the Taconic event, 450 million years ago; and the most recent, the Acadian event, 360 million years ago.[166] All of these events are associated with the closing of the Iapetus Ocean, which would eventually become the Atlantic Ocean. The opening of the ocean 175 million years ago split the supercontinent Pangaea apart, with some now in North America and other parts found in Europe and Africa. These parts of the supercontinent are now celebrated by the International Appalachian Trail that circles the northern Atlantic following the force, by trail, that shaped the mountains. One of the more interesting things about this location is that researcher Robert Neuman was the first to find evidence of this separation in the small fossils of fan-shaped feeding patterns in the mud stone of Grand Pitch—only one of a handful of locations around these mountains[167] where evidence can be found. The area around Grand Pitch represents one of the most complete exposures of Paleozoic rocks spanning 150 million years, from the stratified Cambrian rocks of the Grand Pitch formation in the northeast to Ordovician volcanics, Silurian and Devonian sedimentary rocks and the Devonian volcanic rocks of the Traveler rhyolite—all containing many well-preserved fossil occurrences for dating.[168]

The final shaping of the monument ended only around twelve thousand years ago; when the last glaciation period ended, the ice melted and the ground rebounded. At its peak, the ice covered the land completely, slowly moving to the southeast, grinding the bedrock as it traveled. When it melted, it left a number of different landforms that in many cases have remained untouched in the monument. It left a general covering of glacial till or drift that was composed of fragments transported by the glacial ice and left behind when it melted, covering the ground in layers of rounded, worn rocks. One type of drift field where the till is a bit more organized is called a ribbed moraine, which can be found in several locations in the monument—there's a large field of ribbed moraines near the north entrance to the monument. They are regularly spaced small ridges believed by some researchers to form near the edge of the glacier as it stopped and moved and stopped again.[169] There are also other interesting and unique features related to surface geology that can be found throughout the monument. Limestone deposits, rock formations, surface features—they are evidence of the past, even the location of where the rivers in the monument started after the glacial period ended. Each of these features tells the visitor something unique about the monument and its formation.

One of the rock formations is called the Owen Brook Limestone. During the early years of the Great Northern Paper Company, it built its mill near the primary resource: the forests. But it was always looking for less expensive materials used in the paper making process. It was in the 1940s that the discovery of limestone erratics along the Wassataquoik Stream stimulated prospecting as far south as the Wassataquoik Stream and north to the Traveler mountains. Limestone was one of the essential ingredients in older pulp production processes, and the Great Northern Paper Company primary source was 125 miles away in Union, Maine. But it was not until 1963, in the course of geological mapping, that the outcrop was finally discovered, making it only twelve miles from Millinocket. But by this time, the paper making process had changed, and the limestone was no longer needed.

The Owen Brook Limestone is an outcrop of calcareous bedrock located west of the Penobscot East Branch containing fossil brachiopods and corals, indicating that the limestone is from the late Silurian age.[170] The Owen Brook Limestone outcrop is distributed in a three-square-mile area bounded on the east by the East Branch of the Penobscot River and on the south by Owen Brook, a minor tributary of the East Branch. The surrounding rock indicates that the limestone is a fault block formation that was formed by the movement of large crustal blocks when forces in Earth's crust pulled it apart. Some parts of Earth were pushed upward, while others collapsed down. The area is poorly drained, being low swampy terrain, topographically controlled by hummocky blocks of limestone outcrop. Deasey Mountain, which rises steeply above the swampy lowland, is underlain by resistant mafic volcanics, making a pattern of sharp relief north and west of the limestone.[171]

It was calculated that the 2.5-million-ton deposit could be produced and then shipped over rough road to Stacyville and the railyard. It was concluded the presence of a considerable tonnage of high-calcium limestone in the form of a steeply dipping coral reef lying on the southwestern flank of a Silurian volcanic sequence may have been of significance as a source of agricultural limestone for the dairy and potato farms of northern and central Maine if it was ever needed.[172] The distance and better methods of transportation were the primary reasons why this deposit prospect was never quarried. You can still see the locations where testing pits for mining were completed, while the upper exposed limestone formation is highly fossiliferous, including many invertebrate phyla. The area is of interest because the limestone has been worn down by a small brook passing through a ridge. This limestone feature has an extremely smooth surface, and fossils can easily be seen in the rock. Because the area is swampy, there is water flowing through the formation even in extremely dry weather, yet at the edge of the formation the water disappears into the ground. With this small limestone canyon, there is evidence that shows how the limestone has dissolved and slowly settled in the area, leaving weathered cracks in the exposed bedrock. The corduroy road through the Hemlock swampy land that once accessed this area can still be seen.

Haskell Rock, one of the most photographed features in the monument, is a conglomerate outcrop in the middle of the river that was deposited about 450 million years ago. *Eric Hendrickson photograph.*

Haskell Rock is another formation that is located in the middle of the river in rapidly moving water. The rock was first described in literature in 1839 by the agriculturalist Ezekiel Holmes, who listed it as "puddingstone," an earlier term for conglomerate, among the rocks of this area.[173] In 1862, the geologist Charles H. Hitchcock mentioned "a very coarse conglomerate" in T5 R8—the earliest of the geologic explorations of Maine to make note of this distinctive rock.[174] This conglomerate, deposited about 450 million years ago, contains volcanic and sedimentary stones of various sizes and occurs in outcrops and boulders in several other locations in the area, both in the rivers and on the land surrounding the river. The conglomerate outcrop can be traced to its original location, having traveled for some distance from the northeast to the southwest area of the river, which indicates that the pillar in the stream is an erosional remnant of a more extensive bedrock unit somewhere to the north.[175] Many boulders of the conglomerate, broken from the underlying bedrock by the force of glacier ice or river flow, are scattered about the river in this vicinity. Haskell Rock, the twenty-foot-tall pillar in the middle of the river, is located about halfway down the pitch.

The river tells the story of the times when it was an area of transition from volcanic islands—Traveler Mountain, the largest volcano in Maine—to underwater sedimentation. Many of the boulders along this section of river are conglomerate and were broken from the underlying bedrock by the force of the glacier and moved around by the flow of the river. Mother Nature has used the forces of the early spring river flow to slowly eat away at the pillar. Looking at the rock, one can see that the force of the water has worn a deep, wide gouge in the middle of the rock. Erosional forces have been most effective when the water was two or three feet above the normal river level, either due to higher stream velocity at flood stage or perhaps to the force of ice jams. Haskell Rock is perhaps the most photographed feature found within the monument. Only time will tell how much longer this unique feature will still be standing, but small cobbles are visible in the conglomerate in most photos. How long it will stand before it tumbles into the river?

Another feature that is found on the very top of Lunksoos Mountain is a rock formation known as pillow lava. What makes the pillow lava at the top of Lunksoos Mountain so special? This is evidence of a dynamic period of volcanic islands in a shallow sea where the pillow lava was formed. According to geologist Robert Neuman, the top of Lunksoos Mountain was formed from when an undersea volcano erupted 450 million years ago during the Ordovician period.[176] Pillow lava contains characteristic pillow-shaped structures that can be attributed to the extrusion of lava under water. During this period of extensive volcanic activity, not all the lava came in the form of the great explosions; some seeped out small vents. What happens is that lava comes up out of a small vent in Earth's crust on the sea floor, and the outside starts to harden because the sea water is cold. There is a large difference in temperature between the lava and the water, and the surface of the emergent tongue cools very quickly, forming a thin skin. While the middle remains fluid, it takes longer to harden, so the magma keeps getting pushed out. The pressure on the hardened lava causes it to blow up like a balloon. As it becomes larger, the outside becomes thicker until finally the pillow can no longer increase in size. The increased pressure causes the pillow to form a small side vent, and another pillow is formed. The process forms fields of these pillows and continues to grow until the flow of lava stops for some reason. So the process always has new pillows formed over the earlier formed pillows. While pillow lava is considered to be all fine grain, there is a difference. The skin cools much faster than the inside of the pillow, so it is very fine grained, with a glassy texture. The magma inside the pillow cools more slowly, so it is slightly coarser than the skin. While the pillow lavas at the top of Lunksoos have undergone extensive glaciation, they can still be identified when visiting the summit.

Throughout the monument, you can find one of the most prominent features of a glacier: large boulders spread in a random manner. When

The monument is filled with these boulders, traveling from the northwest. They are known as erratics, or ice-rafted boulders, finally coming to rest as the glacier melted. *Eric Hendrickson photograph.*

the continental glacier covered the monument with thousands of feet of ice, as it moved it carried materials both large and small with it. Soft rock was ground into a fine powder called glacial clay, but the harder materials were carried along with the ice. These boulders are known as erratics, or ice rafted boulders. Glacial erratic is generally defined as a rock that differs from the type of rock native to the area where it is resting. The name *erratic* in Latin comes from the word *errare*, meaning to wander, and these rocks can be carried to the area from hundreds of miles away. If the rock is simply broken from the bedrock by the glacier and pushed only a short distance, it is known as a drift boulder.[177] If the rock is broken from the side of a cliff later and forms a pile of rocks, some of which may be huge, it is known as talus. As the glacier travels, it picks up these rocks, and then they are rolled and ground into the bedrock below. If the rocks are softer than the bedrock, they are ground into smaller rocks that become a mass known as glacial drift, which covers most of the monument. But if the rocks within the glacier are harder than the underlying bedrock, they will leave grooves and scratches known as glacial striations. These marks in the rock can indicate the direction of the ice movement from long ago. As the ice moved up over ridges of rock, it would take the tops and break them off, depositing them on the lower side as the glacier moved. Once the glacier stopped moving, the ice slowly melted, depositing the rounded boulders where you see them today. There are several locations within the monument where the glacial boulders remain scattered across open ledges, just as they were dropped by the glacier long ago. As you explore the monument and see these large rocks randomly scattered, imagine the force that it took to move them and then look for evidence of the glacier's movement.

Another surface feature found throughout the monument is the glacial esker. In 1861, Charles H. Hitchcock wrote that these "curious ridges are found in great abundance in Maine, and scarcely occur out of state, which are known by the provincial name of horsebacks. We are not ready to theorize upon their origin." Well, things have changed a bit in the years that followed, and scientists now realize that eskers were formed by the meltwater of the glacier and are one of the most recognizable features of the land. But while there are many across the state of Maine, most have been quarried for their sorted gravel; within the monument, they generally have remained untouched. An esker could be thought of as an under-ice river draining the melting glacier through a natural tunnel, with the water under tremendous pressure due to the weight of the ice above it. The sand, gravel and small boulders were deposited and sorted by meltwater streams in tunnels under the decaying ice of the glacier, with the sediments generally well stratified versus the glacial till, which is more chaotic in nature. The snaking ridge of an esker was a great place for the early loggers to build a road because it was relatively flat with good, well-drained soil. Within the esker, the sediments are generally cross-bedded in a manner that allows scientists to determine the velocity of the flow and direction of the glacial movement. The esker generally followed the retreat of the glacier. While eskers are easily segmented and often discontinuous, caused by falling blocks of ice or cross erosion, the materials within the esker have allowed the segments to be connected, making them easily followed through the monument.

The most important esker found in the monument is called the Katahdin Esker, and sections of it can be found along the west side of the river in the Oxbow area and along much of the Wassataquoik Stream's south side. The esker along the Wassataquoik takes a sharp southern turn and is crossed at the beginning of the loop road. This esker has been traced to the coast in Washington County near Columbia, forming what is known as Pineo Ridge Delta, known for the Epping Survey. Remember that the esker is a record of

Talus caves, formed by the movement of the last ice sheet, are found in the monument in a number of different locations. *Eric Hendrickson photograph.*

the intense effects of climate change that have given rise to the land of the monument as we know it today.

The movement of the glacier has caused the tops of ridges to be pushed over, creating a formation called a talus cave. While the monument is not a cavers' destination, it does have some interesting and unique cave features. With the exception of Owen Brook formation, the caves in the monument are talus formed, generally on the south side of rock outcrops, due to the southerly movement of the last glacier. On the southern slopes of Deasey Mountain, you will find an outcrop of Silurian coral reef limestone. There is evidence of a collapsed cave, small shelter caves and other limestone features located in a highly fossiliferous limestone. In the north of the monument, on the south face of Billfish Mountain, there are several small talus caves that were formed in the Traveler rhyolite. What make these small caves unique is the formation of white "coral" speleothems, small stalactites and bacon-type formations within the caves. Just to the north of Little Messer Pond, you will find a unique formation. The caves are formed in conglomerate rock, broken by the glacier from what had formed during the transition from volcanic islands to an ocean with underwater sedimentation. The caves are formed in an erosional remnant of a more extensive bedrock unit. The floor, walls and ceiling of the cave are composed of rounded conglomerate rocks that have traveled some distance. The Lookout Talus Caves were formed as the glacier pushed up and over a granite ridge, breaking off the top and depositing the sections on the south slope near the top of the ridge. While the caves are not large, they offer a unique view into the surface geology of the monument.

Researchers have been able to determine where the Penobscot River became reborn—where it first started to flow again after the glacier retreated and when the river finally reformed. Today, it is thought that the Penobscot River starts in far northern Maine and continues far out into the ocean underwater in the Gulf of Maine. But that was not always the case. During the Pleistocene epoch, the Laurentide ice sheet, which was the last ice sheet, was forming and slowly flowed in a southeasterly direction from the northern part of Baxter State Park across the monument.[178] The ice sheet started to grow forty thousand years ago, reaching its peak around eighteen thousand years ago and finally disappearing from Maine around twelve thousand years ago.[179] At its peak, the ice sheet extended far out over the continental shelf, with the ice having a thickness of more than two miles. Imagine the weight of this ice on the land, depressing the ground into the plastic mantle below.[180] As the ice sheet melted, the water returned to the valleys; at that time, most of the water was locked up in the ice sheet. The melting ice allowed the surface to rebound to its original height. But the rebound of the land and the melting of the ice did not happen at the same rate. The ice melted much more quickly than the surface rebounded. Think of the surface of the earth as a memory foam mattress: when you lie on it, you depress the surface, but when you get up it doesn't pop right back into shape, as it takes a bit of time to rebound. The depressed mattress slowly returns to its original shape, just as the earth's surface slowly rebounded.

When the glacier began retreating from Maine about fifteen thousand years ago, the ice sheet was in contact with the ocean. Just as Maine's coast today has many inlets and estuaries, so, too, did the coast during this melting period.[181] At the same time, the ice melted, causing the sea level to increase due to the added water; the land was slowly rebounding. As the ice retreated inland, the sea was able to invade the river valley, which was in contact with the retreating ice; the gray in the map seen here represents the areas that

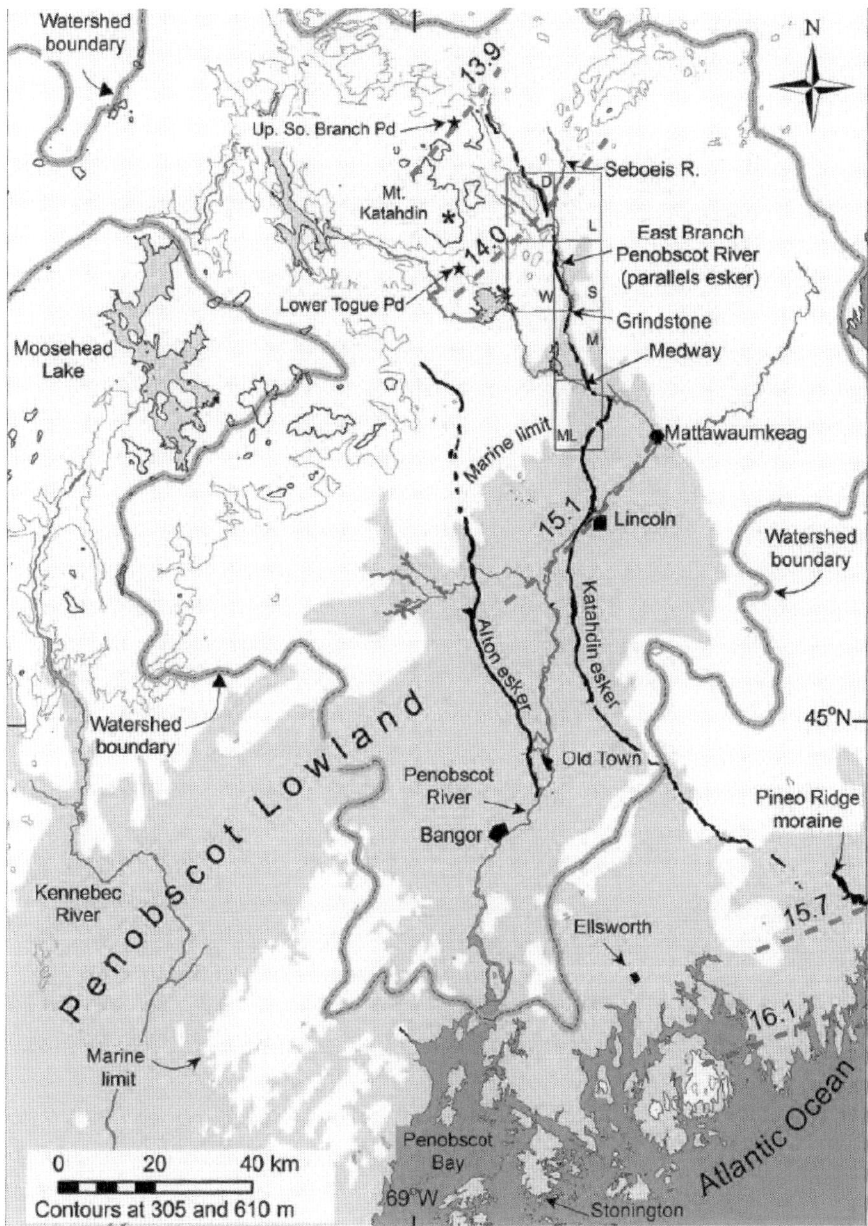

This map by Dr. Robert Hooke shows how far the water from the ocean made it up the Penobscot Valley, allowing scientists to determine where the river was reborn.

were covered by sea water.[182] There were small rivers that flowed into the estuary, forming deltas, just as it does in the ocean today. The deltas are easily recognized by the sandy nature of their makeup. There were three important deltas that formed during this period: the one at the location of the Hunt Farm, which is slowly being eroded by the spring floods; the deltas on both sides of where Sandbank Stream flows into the river, giving its name; and the large Seboeis Delta near the mouth of the stream by the same name.

As the ice melted and the sea level increased, the waters in the estuary raced inland. But there was a point where the rebound of the earth's surface finally caught the sea moving inland, and fourteen thousand years ago the East Branch of the Penobscot River was once again able to flow into the sea. The location of the coming together of all three criteria for the rebirth of the river (melting ice, sea level rise and rebound of the bedrock) was very near where the Seboeis River meets the East Branch of the Penobscot, thus the Seboeis Delta was formed.[183] The melting ice was not uniform, as it would increase and decrease, causing the level of the sea to change. But at its maximum level, the sea would have filled the valley following the East Branch as far upstream as the mouth of the Seboeis River. At that point, the river valley that was once under water would have resurfaced due to the rebound, allowing the river to once again flow into the sea. Imagine, if you will, the Lunksoos and Hunt Farm locations under the sea and Sandbank Stream and the Wassataquoik flowing into the ocean. So, when and where was the East Branch of the Penobscot reborn? The river was reborn fourteen thousand years ago near the mouth of the Seboeis River and has been flowing into the ocean since then.

Between the geology, recent logging, forest fires and beaver working, the monument has still managed to remain wild. It is these activities that have made this area so special. There have been twenty-four different plant communities identified by ecologists within the monument.[184] The most recent logging activity has been carried on by the beavers and is evident in many places throughout the monument. Human logging over the past one hundred years is still evident throughout the area. While there is not much evidence left from before the great 1903 fire, you can still see trees that were burned during that fire throughout the area. There are still some locations within the monument that have forest that has never been cut, as the great fire mineralized the soils in the monument west of the river. What this means for the monument visitor is that there's an incredible number of what are known as small- to medium-size patch ecosystems or plant communities.

One unique community found along the river is called the Silver Maple Flood Plain, which is a very peaceful section to float down, with the trees hanging over the river. The explorer can find these natural features on the upper section of the river known as the Oxbow or along the edge of Haskell Deadwater; in the southern section of the river, they can be found from above Lunksoos Stream to the area below the Hunt Farm all along the river. These floodplains are easily identified by the large silver maple trees hanging over the river. The land itself is very flat, having no understory, and it may even appear as a city park with its large silver maples.[185] Many of the trees are eighty to one hundred feet tall, with a diameter of up to five feet; their trunks are often separated into four or five upright stems, but there are few if any small trees. The floodplain is covered with water for several weeks each spring. The soil is composed of fine sand or silt and has good water drainage, allowing high levels of nutrients from sediments that are deposited during the annual floods. The rich soils are ideal for the growth of the fiddlehead fern or ostrich fern. While the floodplain is beautiful to float through in the summer, it becomes most spectacular in the fall, with the lower water and the leaves changing color and falling into the river to float along beside you.

CHAPTER 11

WATERS AND WETLANDS OF THE MONUMENT

One of the preeminent natural features of Katahdin Woods and Waters National Monument would have to be the East Branch of the Penobscot River system, including its two major tributaries, the Seboeis River and Wassataquoik Stream. The twenty-six-mile stretch of river between Matagamon Bridge just below the dam and the Whetstone Bridge, the East Branch of the Penobscot River, runs free with no bridges or dams. You can look at this section of the river as three distinctly different parts. In the first stretch, for the ten miles from Matagamon Dam to Bowlin Brooks, the river drops more than two hundred feet over a series of spectacular rapids and waterfalls, and several small brooks enter the river. For the second stretch, the ten miles from Bowlin Brook to the mouth of the Seboeis River, it only drops eighty feet, with its major tributaries on the west of Big Spring Brook and Traveler Brook flowing off the side of Traveler Mountain and Little Spring Brook flowing out of the mountains in the center of the monument; the tributaries on the east are Lunksoos Stream and Fiske Brook. For the last stretch, the six miles to Whetstone Bridge, the river drops only twenty five feet but has Seboeis River flowing in from the east and the Wassataquoik Stream flowing in from the west, as well as the small streams Owens Brook, Sandbank Stream and Soldier Brook.

Other streams in the monument would include Sandy Stream and Mud Brook to the west and Shin Brook and a number of smaller brooks to the east. If we look at the Wassataquoik Stream, it is about as remote as can

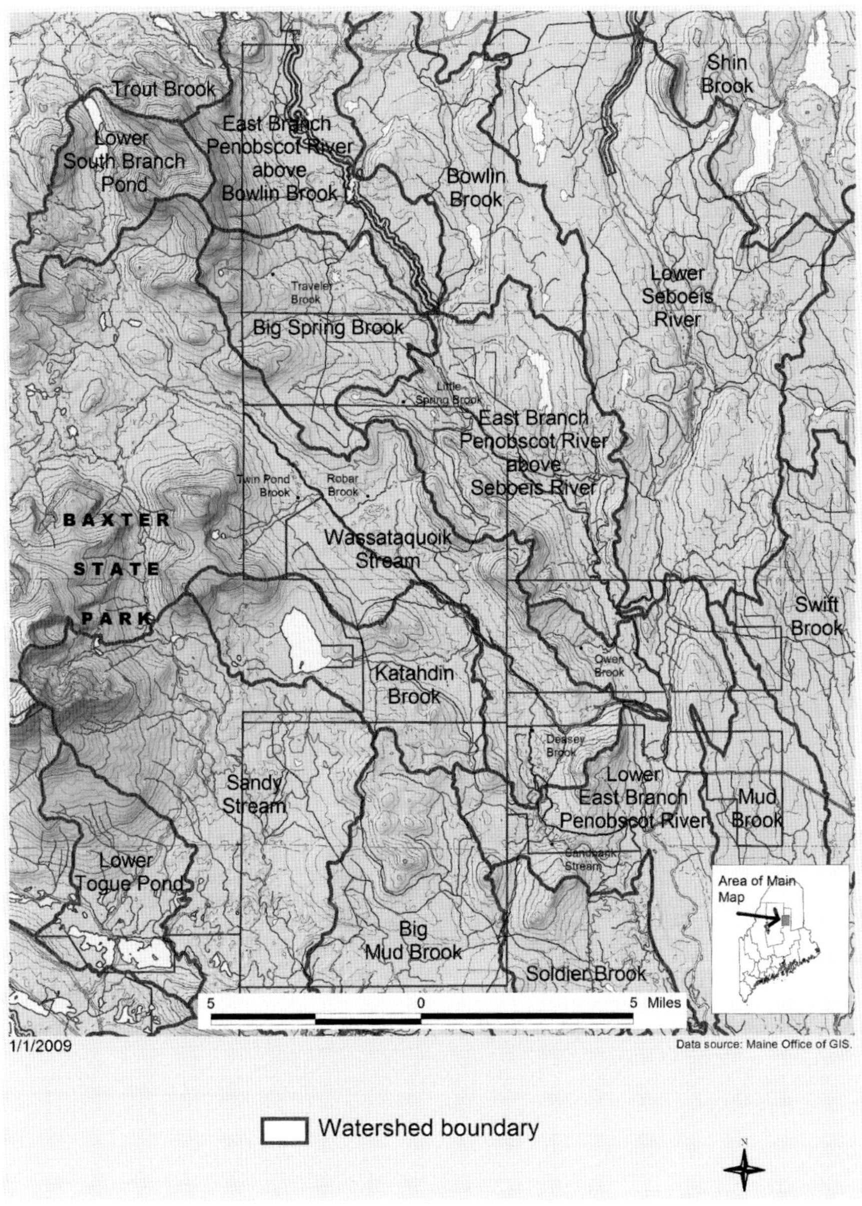

This map by Bart DeWolf shows the watersheds within the monument and how they are related.

be, flowing from the Klondike in the center of Baxter Sate Park to the East Branch of the Penobscot and dropping more than five hundred feet over fourteen miles in almost continuous rapids formed by glacial boulders. The flow is increased with the addition of Twin Pond Brook, Katahdin Brook and Deasey Brook to the south, with Robar Brook to the north. In the southwest corner of the monument, you will find Sandy Stream and Mud Brook, which flow into Millinocket Lake and then into the West Branch of the Penobscot River.

The natural beauty of the valley of the East Branch of the Penobscot River and its tributaries has been recognized in various natural resource studies done by both the State of Maine and the federal government. A study in the 1970s found the East Branch of the Penobscot River suitable for inclusion in the National Wild and Scenic Rivers System. The 1982 National Park Service did the Maine Rivers Study, which listed the East Branch system, including Seboeis River and Wassataquoik Stream, among its A-ranked rivers, declaring it to be one of the least developed watersheds in the Northeast.[186]

There are very few lakes and ponds within the monument feeding the rivers, but there are a number of other wetlands that do add a steady flow of water to the rivers and streams. Within the monument, the wetlands are the link between the land and water and are considered to be some of the most productive ecosystems in the world. There are several types of wetland there: swamps, marshes, bogs and fens; there are also vernal pools that are seasonal wetlands. Depending on the type of wetland, they can be filled with trees, grasses, shrubs or mosses. By definition, to be called a wetland, the area must be filled or soaked with water at least part of the year, with some wetlands actually being dry at certain times of year.[187]

While the monument has all of the different types of wetlands, each is different and creates a unique ecosystem offering a wide variety of plant communities. Most people just call them all swamps and try to avoid them altogether, not realizing the beauty they are missing. Wetlands are simply physical features that act like natural sponges by holding floodwater and the winter melted snow and then slowly releasing the water over time, keeping rivers at normal levels. Wetlands are ecosystems with water tables that are at the soil surface. Wetlands filter and purify the water as it moves through the system, while at the same time the plants within the wetlands control erosion.[188]

The two common wetlands that most people understand are the marsh and the swamp. A swamp is a wetland that is dominated by forest and often

There a number of fens found in the monument, peatlands that are rich in nutrients and feature flowing water. *Eric Hendrickson photograph.*

occurs along ponds or rivers; they can most commonly be seen around beaver working within the monument. These can be found in many locations, even in unexpected areas. A marsh, on the other hand, is a wetland that is dominated by grasses, cattails and small non-woody plants and is commonly found along the banks of a river. The difference between a swamp and a marsh is that swamps have trees, while marshes have only smaller plants, generally grasses.

But the more important wetland features of the monument would be the bogs and fens.[189] In Maine, most people just call them bogs, even when the fens are far more common in this area. Bogs and fens are formed during long anaerobic periods without oxygen, with limited decomposition of organic matter such as plant roots, leaves, stems, mosses and even pollen. Over time, these organic materials build up in layers, often to form peat. Scientists use data collected from these layers to determine information about past climate change. The bog is characterized by spongy peat deposits, acidic water and a thick carpet of spongy sphagnum moss. The bog is generally fed only by water from snowmelt and rain rather than runoff and has acidic water with low nutrient levels. The fen is a peatland that is less acidic and extremely rich in nutrients. The water in a fen comes from mineral-rich surface water or groundwater. So, a bog and fen differ first in their source water. Bog water comes from precipitation, making it acidic, and is nutrient poor, while a fen is fed by either groundwater or surface water, making it less acidic and nutrient rich. Bogs and fens are important to the ecosystem because the gradual accumulation of the decayed plant materials is a natural carbon sink.[190] In the north of the monument, you will find a number of kettle hole bogs—many are dry in the summer, making them vernal pools—as well as large number of beaver swamps. You will even have a chance to drive through a fen in the southern monument just past Mile 3 on the loop road.

One of the unique fens is found in the northern part of the monument. Along the edge of the road going to Haskell Gate, you will find a seven-acre section of land known as "Mother Nature's Garden." The area is lush green in summer and has a wide variety of wild flowers and ferns.[191] When the last ice age was coming to an end twelve thousand years ago, it made changes to the land that have helped made this area special. As the ice sheet retreated, it left behind large amounts of gravel and small rocks known as glacial till drift covering the area. As the glacier retreated and melted, the edge of the ice sheet started to fall apart, leaving a large block of ice from the glacier that was covered by outwash materials. When the block melted, it left a depression in the ground. This depression, which formed Mother Nature's Garden, was locked in place by an esker to the south, ribbed moraines to the east and north and Traveler Mountain to the west.[192] The depression is known as a kettle hole, slowly filling with rich alluvial soil.[193] The valley to the west on the slopes of Traveler Mountain is a fairly large watershed, and winter snows often melt quickly in the spring, releasing large amounts of water. There are no ponds to hold and slow the flow of the water, so it has to rush down off the side of the mountain, forcing a path through the eskers and moraines to the river. The stream flows through the area and crosses the road and then onto the East Branch of the Penobscot River at the Oxbow. Because the stream fills quickly, it carries all the fine soils down off the side of the mountain into this shallow depression when the flow slows. The soil under the area is composed of small rocks and gravel left by the glacier; it drains quickly, making the stream dry most of the year.

This area became known as Mother Nature's Garden due to these rich soils and the wide variety of perennial wildflowers that grow in the area in the early spring. When you enter the area, the first thing that you notice is that there are no small trees and shrubs. The largest trees are surrounded by smaller ones around the edge of the garden and a few large fallen trees within the garden area. The water washes through the area so rapidly most springs that it removes all the seeds left from the fall. All you have is bare ground in many places and extremely large hardwood trees.[194] But before the maples leaves block the light, spring flowers begin to grow. What this means is that in the early spring, the area explodes with wildflowers and ferns. As the summer progresses, the ferns take over, leaving the rich soils carpeted in a lush green color. While you see mostly large ferns, that doesn't mean that there are no summer flowers—it's just that they are small and well hidden.

Some of the many flowers that can be found in this small area include trout lilies, blood root, the Carolina springbeauty, downy yellow violet, sessile-leaved bellwort and, my favorite, the perennial herbaceous plant Dutchman's breeches. The fertile, moist soils are also home to the ostrich fern, which in its young, unfurled form is better known as the fiddlehead fern or simply fiddlehead. This area of the monument exists due to the unique combination of the effects of the most recent glacial ice sheet and the winter melted snows. The surrounding area is exceptionally well drained, with a complex pattern of small parallel ridges and intervening depressions known geologically as a ribbed moraine field. The depressions host pocket wetlands and provide channels for several of the streams descending from Traveler toward the river.

We have looked at what is in the monument that makes it special, but now let us take a moment to look at what almost happened to the area. In 1908, the USGS undertook a survey of the water resources on the East Branch of the Penobscot River from Grand Lake to Medway to determine where dams might be placed to provide the largest value for the water to the people of Maine and the mills. It started at Grand Lake dam, which was constructed in 1847 as a cribwork dam to hold water for the river drives. As the surveyors went down the river, they placed a number of aluminum markers in the rocks along the river. There is one located at Stair Falls (595.7 feet), one located at Bowlin Falls (446.6 feet), one at the mouth of Little Spring Brook near the federal fish hatchery (401.6 feet), one at the Hunt Farm (352.6 feet) and one at Whetstone Falls now covered by the bridge (340.0 feet). It was these markers that they used to determine where dams could be placed and how much water they would hold; in 1908, there was 230 million board feet of timber cut in the Maine, and it needed to be moved downriver. A gauging station was established on October 23, 1902, near the railroad bridge in Grindstone, so they had a fair understanding of how much water was flowing down the river at any given time.

The recommendations of the report indicated that dams could be constructed and gave specific locations. The first location was about 0.75 mile below a location known as "Devils Hole"; the dam would be 15 feet high and back water up for about 1.25 miles. The dam would be about 1,000 feet long at a point about 0.9 mile below Little Spring Brook, where there could also be a 600-foot dam with a head of 20 feet backing up the water for about 1.3 miles above the dam. At Bowlin Falls, about 1,500 feet below the falls, a 400-foot dam would back the water up all the way to the Hulling Machine Pitch; a 400-foot dam at the head of the Hulling Machine Pitch would have a head of 25 feet, extending all the way to Grand Pitch. The least extensive dam could be constructed at Grand Pitch, with little damage to the forest, backing water up all the way to Pond Pitch. There was a dam at Grand Lake with a 14-foot head used for driving logs that was constructed between two ledge outcrops; it was a timber crib dam 185 feet long with five 8-foot gates and one sluice gate of 17 feet to drive logs. The report indicated

Matagamon Dam was a log crib dam built in 1847; it was flooded and replaced by the current dam in 1941, built just downstream. *Patten Lumbermen's Museum.*

that increasing the head by 15 feet would hold a tremendous amount of water, as the land above was low and flat.[195] Fortunately, the only dam that was built was the Grand Lake Matagamon Dam, which was constructed in 1941 just downstream from the old crib dam and is currently used for recreational purposes.

Where did the names of the pitches and falls come from in the first place? On the upper reaches of the East Branch of the Penobscot River, in the first ten miles, there are several rapids known to all who would travel the river even today. In the early days, there were two named rapids, the first being Stair Falls and the second, farther downstream, called Grand Falls due to its size. At Stair Falls, the water rushes over a series of peculiar ledge formations that appear to resemble a staircase. When Jonathan Maynard did his survey in 1793, he referred to the falls as Stair Case Falls. The falls travel over a number of small ledge drops, falling about 18 feet over the course of eight-tenths of a mile. The second was called Grand Falls, where the river flows over five named pitches in a two-mile stretch of river where the river drops 212 feet over rapids, pitches and falls.[196]

Starting at the bottom and moving upstream, the first pitch is called Bowlin Pitch, a five-foot drop over a small ledge just above the mouth of Bowlin Brook. The next pitch, about one mile upstream, is called the Hulling Machine Pitch, where the river drops twenty-two feet in a very crooked course between precipitous ledge banks. Folklore tells of how long logs during the river drive would pass through the falls having all their bark ripped off by the rocks in the pitch. The next is called Grand Pitch, where the river drops nineteen feet over an almost sheer drop in a high-walled canyon. The next pitch, moving upstream, is called Pond Pitch, where the water falls about twelve feet over a solid ledge that crosses the river. Behind the ledge, just before the drop is a calm section of water that resembles a small pond, giving it the name Pond Pitch.

The last drop in the series is called Haskell Rock Pitch. This pitch is made up of two distinctively different sections on the river. In the first, going south, the river flows over a series of ledge drops losing thirty-six feet between solid ledge banks before it turns to the east, where the river runs over series of steep rapids, losing seven feet through a section of boulder. It is this second section where you will find Haskell Rock, the twenty-foot-tall pillar in the middle of the river. The story of the name for this one is a set of circumstances of hope followed by disaster. Shortly after Maine became a state, and badly needed money, disaster struck the nation in 1837. The economic panic and recession lasted until 1843.[197] A young William M.

Grand Pitch is the largest drop on the East Branch and is made of the oldest rocks found in the monument. *Kathy Budden Durr photograph.*

Haskell headed into the wilderness to support his family and the Freewill Baptist Church in Poland, which he had just become a member of a few months earlier. It was a late log drive in mid-June 1841, as it had gotten hung up several times before it finally made it to the location in the river with the large rock pillar in the center. The logs were once again jamming the river, with the water building up quickly behind.

Twenty-five-year-old William Haskell's job was to go out on the jam and try to free the logs. This was often done using explosives or moving a log or two and then quickly getting back to shore using a boat or crossing rocks. However, the jam burst suddenly and took William by surprise, giving him no time to make it to shore in the boat. He was quickly washed downstream, surrounded by logs banging off the rocks; about two-thirds of a mile downstream, he became trapped in the spine holes of a wing dam used to direct the logs moving downstream. He drowned, trapped in this dam, on June 19. On July 10, twenty two days after the accident, his father, George Haskell; an Indian guide; and one other man reached the location to find and remove the body. The body was in such a shape that the men made a riverside grave for William near the site of the accident.[198] The rock is named for William M. Haskell, who was drowned here on

June 19, 1841, while breaking a log jam. It was reported in the church news[199] by Pastor James Libby of the Freewill Church in Poland, Maine, on July 21, 1841. His name would become a reminder of the dangerous and difficult lives of the loggers in these woods.

CHAPTER 12

PRESERVATION AND PROCLAMATION

Federal protection for the area, like many other federally protected locations, has a long, controversial history. By 1900, with the lumbermen moving into the area it was realized that something had to be done to protect the wilderness character of the forest before it was completely gone. The protection movement started to the west with the monument's neighbor, the Baxter State Park, a park set aside for the people of Maine as an area to provide a wilderness experience. The area was first promoted to be protected in 1904 by the Federation of Women's Clubs, led by Mrs. Joseph Thompson of Bangor, who urged the state to adopt a project for the acquisition of the Mount Katahdin area as a state park.[200] In 1908, Charles Hichborn, speaking at the Maine State Board of Trade, called for a Katahdin Preserve not unlike the White Mountains Forest Preserve.[201] Complicating matters, in 1900, the Great Northern Paper Company opened a mill in Millinocket, which at the time would become the world's largest producer of paper. To make paper, it needed raw materials, so the company began buying as much land as possible in the northern unorganized townships. To aid in the process of industrialization, the federal government did a survey of the water resources the company controlled in 1908 to determine where power dams might be constructed.[202] As the land was disappearing and good-paying jobs were being created by the company, individuals began to realize that something needed to be done quickly to protect the area before all the wilderness was gone.

In 1911, Maine's Congressman Guernsey presented a bill to create a national park and national forest reserve around Mount Katahdin. It was supported by the Maine legislature in 1913 but never passed. It was once again attempted in 1916 by Congressman Guernsey, but nothing came of it.[203] Perhaps this was due to the fact that Sieur de Monts National Monument was proclaimed by President Woodrow Wilson in July 1916, becoming Lafayette National Park in February 1919, the first national park east of the Mississippi—it was then expanded, renamed Acadia National Park[204] in 1929. In 1916, Percival Baxter would start to become the driving force in the formation of a future state park. Baxter, a powerful force as a Maine representative, became increasingly concerned with the large landholders, such as the Great Northern Paper Company (GNP) or the Coe Estate of Bangor, that already owned 9 percent of the timberland in Maine. There was a battle of words between Garret Schenck of Great Northern Paper and Percival Baxter over his land protection goals. In 1918, the U.S. Forest Service surveyed the area, reporting that 53 percent of the area had been burned, with only 12 percent being uncut forest—the remainder was bare rock, wetlands or lakes. But even with so little productive timber in the area, there was a great deal of opposition to the concept of protection from the Great Northern Paper Company. It did not want to protect the forest in any way, useable or not; even attempts made in 1919 to purchase cut-over or burned-over lands in the area failed. Percival Baxter continued efforts to purchase lands and encourage others to contribute to his cause. On March 3, 1931,[205] Baxter formally donated the parcel with Mount Katahdin to the State of Maine with the condition that it be kept forever wild—from then on, part of the area was under protection for the future.

In 1933, several proposals to create a national forest or national parks were aired. Governor Brann, returning from a planning meeting in Washington, D.C., proposed the creation of a Roosevelt National Park consisting of 1 million acres in the Mount Katahdin region. In December, he asked the legislature to permit the federal government to purchase the lands with $2 million that had been earmarked by the president. The bill was accepted but amended to allow the acquisition by purchase or gift but not by eminent domain and to note that the state would retain the rights to water.[206] It was agreed on a week before Christmas by the state, but it was not satisfactory to the federal government due to water rights. The GNP had fought hard against passage of the measure and wanted those water rights. In 1936, Governor Brann officially requested the National Park Service to investigate the feasibility of establishing a national park in the

Mount Katahdin region. The federal study reported that Mount Katahdin by itself was not sufficiently large to warrant park status but that an area of at least 512 square miles, including the mountain, would be worthy of setting aside.

In July, Earle Pritchard, recreational planner for the NPS, called on Percival Baxter for his views on possible acquisition by the park service for the purchase of the lands and the possibility of the federal agency taking over Baxter State Park. Percival Baxter responded that he did not want the federal government in the region—expecting a long struggle and the long-range planning involved in the future of Baxter State Park.[207] At this point, the idea of a federal park turned to what the federal government could do to help the Baxter State Park using the Civilian Conservation Corps. A federal park of 512 square miles would have included much of what is currently Baxter State Park but not all, much of what makes up the protected part of Katahdin Woods and Waters National Monument and most of the headwaters of the Allagash Wilderness Waterway.[208]

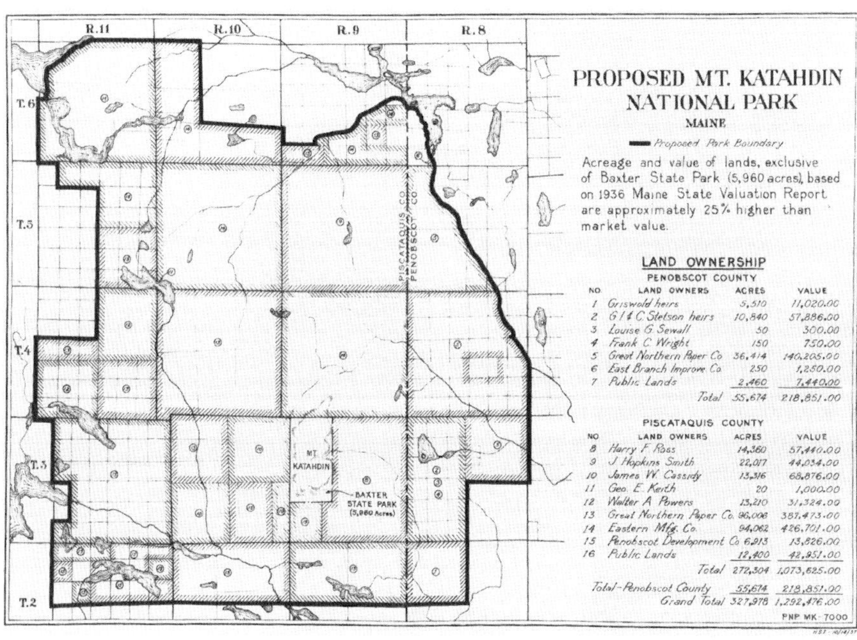

The governor of Maine requested a preliminary study of the Katahdin area by the National Park Service. Representative Brewster of Maine introduced a bill (HR 5864) in Congress. This is the map and costs associated with the proposed park. *Myron Avery Collection, Maine State Library.*

Under Baxter's guidance and land purchases, the Baxter State Park's protected area continued to grow, with the last Baxter purchase coming in 1962 and the last addition to the park coming in 2006 with the Katahdin Lake parcel. In 1988, the National Parks and Conservation Association renewed the call for federal protection surrounding Baxter State Park. The Wilderness Society in 1989 recommended the creation of a 2.7-million-acre Maine Woods Reserve. But the strongest push would come in 1994 when a group called RESTORE proposed the creation of a Maine Woods National Park in the area where Thoreau traveled and called for the national preserve more than 150 years earlier. The proposal called for the protection of 3.2 million acres of Maine's forest, mountains and lakes. The organization gained a great deal more attention than it expected when it published a brochure called *Proposed National Park & Preserve: A Vision of What Could Be.* The brochure was published in the style of the National Park trifolds and was circulated in the Boston area. In many cases, the people of northern Maine found out about the proposal, much to their surprise, when they picked up the trifolds on trips to Boston. The organization met with a great deal of resistance, as the Maine people did not want out-of-staters telling them what to do with their land. RESTORE continued to push for a Maine Woods National Park at every chance. In 1997, Roxanne Quimby, while working at the Common Ground Fair selling beeswax products, became aware of the ambitious plan for the Maine Woods National Park surrounding Baxter State Park; in 2000, she expressed her interest in the organization.

Quimby came to Maine in 1975 from Massachusetts by way of Connecticut and then post-secondary school at the San Francisco Art Institute. She lived in a single-room back-to-nature cabin in Guilford, where she gave birth to twins. She moved out of the cabin, doing various jobs, before meeting a beekeeper named Burt Shavitz. She fell in love with the idea of keeping bees and selling honey, including beeswax products. Her sales of candles, boot and furniture polish and other beeswax products was an instant success. When she added the lip balm, Burt's Bees products was born. The company grew quickly, in part due to her love of nature and the company wanting to leave a lasting environmental legacy through the natural and recycled materials used in her products. In October 2000, she joined the board of RESTORE and began promoting the plan through her products.

Quimby strongly believed that the purchase of any forestland was an exceptional deal, so on August 4, 2000, she purchased[209] her first land for conservation from Herb Haynes and Lakeville Shores, a 2,407-acre parcel bordering the Appalachian Trail near Big Wilson Stream in Elliotsville

Township for $239 per acre. That same day, she purchased 5,800 acres in T8 R11 for $267 per acre known as the Bluffer Parcel; Haynes wanted to cut the parcel of old growth, and local people were fighting to protect the land, so selling it was an easy out for Haynes. Quimby was well on her way to buying land, and her rule was to always pay the willing sellers a fair market price for the land. She considered the purchase of land to be a precious natural treasure. She also realized, just as Baxter had before her, that land that had been cut over was a good deal—the forest value had been removed, but with time, just as in Baxter, the forest would recover. At this point, she would begin to keep her land purchase plans to herself to prevent people from capitalizing on her plans. Still working on the RESTORE plan, she made her third land purchase of 77 acres on June 15, 2001, near Mount Kineo on Moosehead Lake, which was land the state had been trying to purchase unsuccessfully—she was able to purchase it at a cost of $4,550 per acre. At the time, the land was hailed by RESTORE as the gateway to the proposed park, while Quimby wanted it because both Thoreau and Roosevelt had visited it. The purchase and its publicity mobilized the anti-park people throughout the state.

RESTORE had the expectation that Quimby would donate her lands to the organization, but her intent was to donate her lands to the National Park Service or control them in conservation. In public meetings, the resistance to the concept of a park increased, with communities refusing to back the concept. In March 2003, Quimby resigned from the board because she felt she was getting enough resistance on her own and did not need the extra resistance from RESTORE. She tried unsuccessfully to donate her Bluffer Pond Parcel to the Nature Conservancy, but it did not want it because it had been cut over. She strongly believed that she could buy any property from willing sellers in any condition—the more cut over it was, the cheaper the land, and within a few years it would return to the wild that it once was before cutting.

Quimby paid $4 million on March 3, 2004, for the tract in T3 R7 where Sandbank Campground is located that previously was owned by Hancock Timber Resources. Earlier in the year, she had purchased 9,894 acres just to the east of Baxter State Park. On November 24, 2004, Quimby purchased 24,083 acres in T5 R8 at $500 per acre; many local people felt that she would be using this property as an anchor for her park and that they would lose snowmobile access to the main north–south route. The new paradigms came with these purchases because she was not in the log business and did not want her roads used for logging, which had been tradition, thus preventing logging companies from crossing her lands. People were not happy, and criticism of her plan increased, some even sending threatening letters and e-mails. On October 25, 2005, there was a major land swap between Quimby and William Gardner, with land in T5 R8 being swapped for the land north of the Wassataquoik in T4 R8. It was a win-win for both. Quimby stopped a proposed bridge over the pristine Wassataquoik and protected a section of land on the eastern boundary of Baxter State Park, while Gardner got easily accessible land for his cutting operation, Bowlin Camps and the snowmobile trail. But the most important part of the deal was that two completely different people had a meeting of the minds, which would lead to many more deals in the future.

On September 1, 2006, Quimby purchased 23,000 acres in the southern half of T3 R8 and the northern half of T2 R8, which is in the southwest corner of the monument, from Herb H. Haynes and R.A. Crawford for $435 per acre. On April 24, 2007, Quimby purchased 2,683 acres in T4 R7 on the east side or the river and 659 acres from Charles Fitzgerald in T4 R8 up the Wassataquoik. She purchased a parcel of 4,918 acres that included Deasey Ponds and the Hunt Farm in T3 R7 on August 6, 2007. At this point, she owned most of the land on the east side of Baxter State Park, with the exception of a small parcel of land shaped like a piano-key across from Bowlin Camps that Fraser Paper had refused to sell her. At this point, most of timber sellers realized that they could cut as much as the law would allow and Quimby would still purchase the land.

Statewide resistance continued to build as she purchased another 419-acre tract of Fitzgerald land southwest of the Wassataquoik. She also sold the Bluffer Parcel that she had offered to the Nature Conservancy without conservation restrictions for double what she had paid for it six years earlier, which freed up funds for different purchases. In 2011, she finally began to articulate her very clear vision of what she wanted to do with her land by creating a national park and her reasons why she supported the concept. She also made it clear that some leases would be canceled; on others, the prices of the leases would go to fair market value, which caused some leases to go from $25 per year to $1,500 in the first year. She also indicated that hunting, trapping and the use of motorized vehicles would be prohibited on her lands, with gates starting to appear. In January 2011, she sold 5,061 acres to the state in T2 R8 to be called the Millinocket Town Forest and a conservation easement for the Hunt parcel in T3 R8, allowing the state to control the ITS 85 snowmobile trail. On May 9, 2011, in a meeting in Millinocket, Roxanne Quimby finally shared with the public her intent to make her lands a gift to the federal government in 2016, the 100th birthday of the National Park System. In April 2011, she purchased the 13.2-acre Lunksoos parcel where her two loves, art and nature, could come together; also, the purchase was considered to be a tactical move on her part to prevent the property from becoming a commercial business. In January 2014, she purchased a small parcel that would connect a large parcel purchased earlier to Lower Shin Pond. According to Phyllis Austin, she continued to work toward the purchase of a parcel of 900 acres to the south, including Whetstone Bridge, although it never took place because it would connect her properties and control the access to the bridge.

In 2011, Quimby, while doing a phone interview for *Forbes* magazine, made some off-hand statements out of frustration about the people of Maine that enraged the anti-park people and showed up in many Maine publications. By 2012, she had become the eighty-sixth-largest private landholder in the country with ownership of 119,000 acres. On December 10, 2012, she was finally able to purchase the 8,315-acre tract bordering Baxter State Park across from Bowlin Camps with a ridge known as the Lookout. At this point, she realized that she could no longer be the face of the national park effort, so she started to retreat from the public eye; at the same time, her son, Lucas St. Clair, would move from Seattle to Portland and become the new face of the park mission. St. Clair was proud of the fact that he could win people over to the concept one cup of coffee at a time. Slowly, the support for the park began to build, followed by agreements with various groups for their support. He always wanted to know why people opposed the park, and if possible, he would include changes; if not, he would take the time to explain the reason for not making changes. In September 2013, he announced that hunting, snowmobiling and ATV use would be allowed east of the river in what would become called the recreational tract.

In December 2013, Roger Milliken, the president of the Baskahegan Company, a lumbering operation that owned timberlands around Quimby's timberlands, publicly stated that if studies indicated it should become a park, he would support the move. In 2014, things changed and everything was tossed in the air with the closing of the area paper mills; high-paying industrial jobs were gone, and the largest employers in the area would now be Baxter State Park, the hospital and the school system. On August 12, 2016, Roxanne Quimby transferred her lands (13 parcels of various sizes with specific deeds[210]) in the Katahdin region to the federal government. The deeds were filed in Millinocket on August 23, then on August 24, 2016, President Barack Obama designated 87,563 acres east of Baxter State Park as Katahdin Woods and Waters National Monument; the announcement would come one day before the National Park Service turned one hundred years old. In the President's Proclamation there is a summary of what is found in the monument and what really makes it worth becoming a national treasure controlled by the National Park Service.

From the bald summits of Deasey Mountain, Lunksoos Mountain, Hathorn Mountain and Little Spring Brook Mountain, from boreal forests to floodplains along the East Branch of the Penobscot River, you have many unique forest communities. Places like the rock barrens, the cliff-side plant communities and the fens found throughout the monument with their rare flora and fauna. There are trees that range from regeneration to trees more than 250 years old that missed the fire and axe of the logger. The Wassataquoik Stream is special because the water is clear, cool and clean, perfect for aquatic life, while the East Branch of the Penobscot River has its own unique aquatic life. While it will never be the same wilderness that

The remains of an F-86A Sabre that crashed in 1952, killing the pilot, remains a memorial deep in the forest of the monument and should be respected. *Eric Hendrickson photograph.*

There are many artifacts present throughout the monument, such as this boom chain over a log crib. Please do not remove anything found in the monument. Leave them for others to enjoy. *Eric Hendrickson photograph.*

Thoreau, Baxter or Roosevelt experienced, the lands are now protected and preserved to retain the species diversity of plants and animals—reminders of how it was hundreds of years ago. This special patchwork of natural communities has allowed birders to see species where they would never expect to see them.

The Katahdin Woods and Waters National Monument is mandated to protect and preserve all resources, not only for today but also for tomorrow and for the children of the future generations. As such, you are not allowed to remove any natural or cultural objects, including fossils, rocks, historical artifacts, animals or plants. The context that fossils and artifact are found in is extremely important, so they should never be moved. This book is not meant to be a guide to locations but more of a history of what makes this area of Maine so special.

To truly understand the reason why Katahdin Woods and Waters National Monument has come to exist and what makes it so unique, you should take the time to read the proclamation that created the monument on August 24, 2016, by order of President Barack Obama. This is a special place of wilderness forest and rivers that most people across the country would never have a chance to experience if it were not for the monument. This monument will give families a chance to see what happens as an industrial forest is slowly turned back into a wilderness forest. The martin, spruce grouse, moose, black bear and lynx have their own preferred habitats and can be seen throughout the monument by visitors, a testament to its return to a more natural state.

> *Proclamation 9476*
> *Establishment of the Katahdin Woods and Waters National Monument*
> *August 24, 2016*
> *By the President of the United States of America*
>
> *In north central Maine lies an area of the North Woods known in recent years as the Katahdin Woods and Waters Recreation Area* [Katahdin Woods and Waters], *approximately 87,500 acres within a larger landscape already conserved by public and private efforts starting a century ago. Katahdin Woods and Waters contains a significant piece of this extraordinary natural and cultural landscape: the mountains, woods, and waters east of Baxter State Park (home of Mount Katahdin, the northern terminus of the Appalachian Trail), where the East Branch of*

the Penobscot River and its tributaries, including the Wassataquoik Stream and the Seboeis River, run freely. Since the glaciers retreated 12,000 years ago, these waterways and associated resources—the scenery, geology, flora and fauna, night skies, and more—have attracted people to this area. Native Americans still cherish these resources. Lumberjacks, river drivers, and timber owners have earned their livings here. Artists, authors, scientists, conservationists, recreationists, and others have drawn knowledge and inspiration from this landscape.

Katahdin Woods and Waters contains objects of significant scientific and historic interest. For some 11,000 years, Native peoples have inhabited the area, depending on its waterways and woods for sustenance. They traveled during the year from the upper reaches of the East Branch of the Penobscot River and its tributaries to coastal destinations like Frenchman and Penobscot Bays. Native peoples have traditionally used the rivers as a vast transportation network, seasonally searching for food, furs, medicines, and many other resources. Based on the results of archeological research performed in nearby areas, researchers believe that much of the archeological record of this long Native American presence in Katahdin Woods and Waters remains to be discovered, creating significant opportunity for scientific investigation. What is known is that the Wabanaki people, in particular the Penobscot Indian Nation, consider the Penobscot River (including the East Branch watershed) a centerpiece of their culture and spiritual values.

The first documented Euro-American exploration of the Katahdin region dates to a 1793 survey commissioned by the Commonwealth of Massachusetts. After Maine achieved statehood in 1820, Major Joseph Treat, guided by John Neptune of the Penobscot Tribe, produced the first detailed maps of the region. The Maine Boundary Commission authorized a survey of the new State in 1825, for which surveyor Joseph C. Norris, Sr., and his son established the "Monument Line," which runs through Katahdin Woods and Waters and serves as the State's east–west baseline from which township boundaries are drawn.

By the early 19th century until the late 20th century, logging was a way of life throughout the area, as exemplified by the history of logging along the Wassataquoik Stream. To access the upstream forests, a tote road was built on the Wassataquoik's north bank around 1841; traces of the old road can still be seen in places. The earliest loggers felled enormous white pines and then "drove" them down the tumultuous stream.

Beginning in the 1880s, after the choice pines were gone, the loggers switched to spruce long logs, and built camps, depots, and many dams on the Wassataquoik to control its flow for the log drives. Remnants of the Dacey and Robar Dams have been found, and discovery of more logging remnants and historic artifacts is likely. Log driving was dangerous, and many men died on the river and were buried nearby. A large fire in 1884 damaged logging operations on the Wassataquoik, and an even larger fire in 1903 put an end to the long log operations. Pulpwood operations resumed in 1910 but ceased in 1915. Other streams, like Sandy Stream, have similar logging histories.

The East Branch of the Penobscot River and its major tributaries served as a thoroughfare for huge log drives headed toward Bangor. Log drives ended (based primarily on environmental concerns) in the 1970s, after which the timber companies relied on trucking and a network of private roads they started to build in the 1950s.

In the 1800s, the infrastructure that developed to support the logging industry also drew hunters, anglers, and hikers to the area. In the 1830s, within 2 miles of one another on the eastern side of the Penobscot East Branch, William Hunt and Hiram Dacey established farms to serve loggers, which soon also served recreationists, scientists, and others who wanted to explore the Katahdin region or climb its mountains. Just across the East Branch from the Hunt and Dacey Farms (the latter now the site of Lunksoos Camps) lies the entrance to the Wassataquoik Stream. In 1848, the Reverend Marcus Keep established what is still called Keep Path, running along the Wassataquoik to Katahdin Lake and on to Mount Katahdin. From that time until the end of the 19th century, the favored entryway to the Katahdin region started on the east side of Mount Katahdin with a visit to Hunt or Dacey Farm, then crossed the East Branch and ascended the valley of the Wassataquoik Stream.

Henry David Thoreau—who made the "Maine Woods" famous through his publications—approached from the headwaters of the East Branch to the north. With his Penobscot guide Joe Polis and companion Edward Hoar in 1857, on his last and longest trip to the area, he paddled past

Dacey Farm with just a brief stop at Hunt Farm. He wrote about his two nights in the Katahdin Woods and Waters area—the first at what he named the "Checkerberry-tea camp," near the oxbow just upriver from Stair Falls, and the second on the river between Dacey and Hunt Farms where he drank hemlock tea.

During his 1879 Maine trip on which he summited Mount Katahdin, Theodore Roosevelt followed the route across the East Branch and up the Wassataquoik. As Roosevelt later recalled, he lost one of his hiking boots crossing the Wassataquoik but, undaunted, completed the challenging trek in moccasins. Many including Roosevelt himself have observed that his several trips to the Katahdin region in the late 1870s had a significant impact on his life, as he overcame longstanding health problems, gained strength and stamina, experienced the wonder of nature and the desire to conserve it, and made friends for life from the Maine Woods.

Native Mainer Percival P. Baxter, too, followed this route on the 1920 trip that solidified his determination to create a large park from this landscape. Burton Howe, a Patten lumberman, organized this trip of Maine notables, who stayed at Lunksoos Camps before their ascent via the established route. As a State representative, senator, and governor, Baxter had proposed legislation to create a Mount Katahdin park in commemoration of the State's centennial, and the 1920 trip cemented his profound appreciation of the landscape. Spurned by the Maine legislature, Baxter devoted his life to acquiring 28 parcels of land, largely from timber companies who had heavily logged them, and donated them to the State with management instructions and an endowment, resulting in the establishment of Baxter State Park. Artists and photographers have left indelible images of their time spent in the area. In 1832, John James Audubon canoed the East Branch and sketched natural features for his masterpiece Birds of America. *Frederic Edwin Church, the preeminent landscape artist of the Hudson River School, first visited the area in the 1850s, and in 1877 invited his landscape-painter colleagues to join him on a well-publicized expedition from Hunt Farm up the Wassataquoik Stream to capture varied views of Mount Katahdin and environs. In the early 1900s, George H. Hallowell painted and photographed the log drives on the Wassataquoik Stream, and Carl Sprinchorn painted logging activities on the Seboeis River.*

Geologists were among the earliest scientists to visit the area. While surveys were done in the 1800s, in-depth geological research and mapping of the area did not begin until the 1950s. These mid-20th century geologists found bedrock spanning over 150 million years of the Paleozoic era, revealing a remarkably complete exposure of Paleozoic rock strata with well-preserved fossils. The lands west of the Penobscot East Branch are dominated by volcanic and granitic rock from the Devonian period, mostly Katahdin Granite but also Traveler Rhyolite, a light-colored volcanic rock that is similar in composition to granite. The oldest rock in Katahdin Woods and Waters, a light greenish-gray quartzite interlayered with slate from the early Cambrian period (over 500 million years ago), can be observed along the riverbank of the Penobscot East Branch for over 1,000 feet at the Grand Pitch (a river rapid). This rock is part of the Weeksboro–Lunksoos Lake anticline, a broad upward fold of rocks originally deposited horizontally, which is evidence of mountain-building tectonics. The fold continues north along the river and then turns northeast toward Shin Pond, exposing successive bands of younger Paleozoic rock of both volcanic and sedimentary origin on either side of the structure.

Various formations in the area provide striking visual evidence of marine waters in Katahdin Woods and Waters during the geologic periods that immediately followed the Cambrian period. For example, Owen Brook limestone, an outcrop of calcareous bedrock west of the Penobscot East Branch containing fossil brachiopods, is of coral reef origin. Pillow lavas, such as those near the summit of Lunksoos Mountain, were produced by underwater eruptions. Haskell Rock, the 20-foot-tall pillar in the midst of a Penobscot East Branch rapid, is conglomerate bedrock that suggests a time of dynamic transition from volcanic islands to an ocean with underwater sedimentation. This conglomerate, deposited about 450 million years ago, contains volcanic and sedimentary stones of various sizes, and occurs in outcrops and boulders in several locations.

The area's geology also provides prominent evidence of large and powerful earth-changing events. During the Paleozoic era (541 to 252 million years ago), mountain-building events contributed to the rise of the primordial Appalachian Mountain range and the amalgamation of the supercontinent Pangaea. Following the last mountain-building event, significant erosion reshaped the topography, helping to expose the cores of volcanoes, the Katahdin pluton, and the structure of the previous mountain-building events. About 200 million years ago, Pangaea began splitting apart as the Atlantic Ocean appeared and North America, Europe, and Africa formed. Today, the International Appalachian Trail, a long-distance hiking trail, seeks to follow the ancestral Appalachian-Caledonian Mountains on both sides of the Atlantic, starting at Katahdin Lake in Baxter State Park near the northern end of the domestic Appalachian Trail, traversing Katahdin Woods and Waters for about 30 miles, and proceeding through Canada for resumption across the Atlantic.

In more recent geological history, during the approximately 2.5 million year-long Pleistocene epoch that ended approximately 12,000 years ago, repeated glaciations covered the region, eroding bedrock and shaping the modern landscape. Glacial till from the most recent glaciations underlies much of the area's soil, moraines occur in several locations, and glacial erratics are common. Prominent eskers—long, snaking ridges of sand and gravel deposited by glacial meltwater—occur along most of the Penobscot East Branch and the Wassataquoik Stream. Glacial landforms, glacial scoured bedrock, and the lake sediments in the area, deposited only since the retreat of the last glaciers, record a history of intense climate change that gave rise to the modern topography of the area.

This post-glacial topography is studded with attractive small mountains, including some like Deasey, Lunksoos, and Barnard, that offer spectacular views of Mount Katahdin. Katahdin Woods and Waters abuts much of Baxter State Park's eastern boundary, extending the conservation landscape through shared mountains, streams, corridors for plants and animals, and other natural systems.

Among the defining natural features of Katahdin Woods and Waters is the East Branch of the Penobscot River system, including its major tributaries, the Seboeis River and the Wassataquoik Stream, and many smaller tributaries. Known as one of the least developed watersheds in the northeastern United States, the Penobscot East Branch River system has a stunning concentration of hydrological features in addition to its significant geology and ecology. From the northern boundary of Katahdin Woods and Waters, the main stem of the East Branch drops over 200 feet in about 10 miles through a series of rapids and waterfalls—including Stair Falls, Haskell Rock Pitch, Pond Pitch, Grand Pitch, the Hulling Machine, and Bowlin Falls.

After Bowlin Brook, the main stem declines more gently south toward Whetstone Falls and below, embroidered with many side channels and associated floodplain forests and open stream shores. Of the two major tributaries, the Seboeis River flows in from the east, and the Wassataquoik Stream from the west, the latter dropping over 500 feet in its approximately 14-mile wild run from the border of Baxter State Park to its confluence with the Penobscot East Branch main stem.

The extraordinary significance of the Penobscot East Branch River system has long been recognized. A 1977 Department of the Interior study determined that the East Branch of the Penobscot River, including the Wassataquoik Stream, qualifies for inclusion in the National Wild and Scenic Rivers System based on its outstandingly remarkable values, and a 1982 Federal-State study of rivers in Maine determined that the Penobscot East Branch River System, including both the Wassataquoik Stream and the Seboeis River, ranks in the highest category of natural and recreational rivers and possesses nationally significant resource values.

In recent years, a multi-party public-private project has taken steps to reconnect the Penobscot River with the sea through the removal and retrofitting of downstream dams. This river restoration will likely further enhance the integrity of the Penobscot East Branch river system and provide opportunities for scientific study of the effects of the restoration on upstream areas within Katahdin Woods and Waters. It will also allow federally endangered Atlantic salmon to return to the upper reaches of the river known in the Penobscot language as "Wassetegweweck," or "the place where they spear fish." The return of ocean-run Atlantic salmon to this watershed would complement the exceptional native brook trout fishery for which Katahdin Woods and Waters is known today. Katahdin Woods and Waters possesses significant biodiversity. Spanning three ecoregions, it displays the transition between northern boreal and southern broadleaf deciduous forests, providing a unique and important opportunity for scientific investigation of the effects of climate change across ecotones. The forests include mixed hardwoods like sugar maple, beech, and yellow birch; mixed forests with hardwoods, hemlock, and white pine; and spruce-fir forests with balsam fir, red spruce, and birches. In wetland areas, black spruce, white spruce, red maple, and tamarack dominate.

Although significant portions of the area have been logged in recent years, the regenerating forests retain connectivity and provide significant biodiversity among plant and animal communities, enhancing their ecological resilience. With the complex matrix of microclimates represented, the area likely contains the attributes needed to sustain natural ecological function in the face of climate change and provide natural strongholds for species into the future. These forests also afford connections and scientific comparisons with the forests on adjacent State land, including Baxter State Park, which was logged heavily before its parcel-by-parcel purchase by former Governor Percival Baxter between 1931 and 1963.

Of particular scientific significance are the number and quality of small- and medium-sized patch ecosystems throughout the area, tending to occur in less common topography that is often relatively remote or inaccessible. Hilltops and barrens often protect rare flora and fauna, such as the blueberry-lichen barren and associated spruce-heath barren found between Robar and Eastern Brooks, and the three-toothed cinquefoil-blueberry low summit bald atop Lunksoos Mountain, where rattlesnake hawkweed can be found. Cliffs and steep slopes, like those present along the ridge from Deasey Mountain to Little Spring Brook Mountain and on the eastern sides of Billfish and Traveler Mountains, harbor exemplary rock outcrop ecosystems that often include flora of special interest, such as fragrant cliff wood-fern and purple clematis. Ravines and coves can support enriched forests like the maple-basswood-ash community found below the eastern cliffs of Lunksoos Mountain, with trees over 250 years old and associated rare plants including squirrel-corn. The Appalachian-Acadian Rivershore ecosystems of the Penobscot East Branch and its two major tributaries are considered exemplary in Maine, with occurrences of beautiful silver maple floodplain forest and hardwood river terrace forest—rare and imperiled natural communities, respectively, in the State. A nationally significant diversity of high quality wetlands and wet basins occurs throughout Katahdin Woods and Waters, including smaller streams and brooks, ponds, swamps, bogs, and fens. Patch forests of various types also occur throughout the area, such as a red-pine woodland forest on small hills and ridges amid the large Mud Brook Flowage wetland in the southwestern section.

The expanse of Katahdin Woods and Waters, augmented by its location next to other large conservation properties including Baxter State Park and additional State reservations, supports many wide-ranging wildlife species including ruffed grouse, moose, black bear, white-tailed deer, snowshoe hare, American marten, bobcat, bald eagle, northern goshawk, and the federally threatened Canada lynx. Seventy-eight bird species are known to breed in the area, and many more bird species use it. Visitation and study of the area have been limited to date, as compared with other areas like Baxter State Park, and many more species of birds and other wildlife may be present.

Certain wildlife species are known to occur in specific patch ecosystems in the area, such as the short-eared owl in hilltops and barrens, and the silver-haired bat and the wood turtle in floodplain forests. Mussels such as the tidewater mucked and yellow lamp mussel live in some of the brooks and streams, and rare invertebrates like the copper butterfly, pygmy snake tail dragonfly, Tomah mayfly, and Roaring Brook mayfly inhabit some of its bogs and fens.

Katahdin Woods and Waters' daytime scenery is awe-inspiring, from the breadth of its mountain-studded landscape, to the channels of its free-flowing streams with their rapids, falls, and quiet water, to its vantages for viewing the Mount Katahdin massif, the "greatest mountain." The area's night skies rival this experience, glittering with stars and planets and occasional displays of the aurora borealis, in this area of the country known for its dark sky.

Whereas, section 320301 of title 54, United States Code (known as the "Antiquities Act"), authorizes the President, in his discretion, to declare by public proclamation historic landmarks, historic and prehistoric structures, and other objects of historic or scientific interest that are situated upon the lands owned or controlled by the Federal Government to be national monuments, and to reserve as a part thereof parcels of land, the limits of which shall be confined to the smallest area compatible with the proper care and management of the objects to be protected;

Whereas, for the purpose of establishing a national monument to be administered by the National Park Service, Elliotsville Plantation, Inc. (EPI), has donated certain lands and interests in land within Katahdin Woods and Waters to the Federal Government;

Whereas, the Roxanne Quimby Foundation has established a substantial endowment with the National Park Foundation to support the administration of a national monument;

Whereas, Katahdin Woods and Waters is an exceptional example of the rich and storied Maine Woods, enhanced by its location in a larger protected landscape, and thus would be a valuable addition to the Nation's natural, historical, and cultural heritage conserved and enjoyed in the National Park System;

Whereas, it is in the public interest to preserve and protect the historic and scientific objects in Katahdin Woods and Waters;

Now, Therefore, I, Barack Obama, President of the United States of America, by the authority vested in me by section 320301 of title 54, United States Code, hereby proclaim the objects identified above that are situated upon lands and interests in lands owned or controlled by the Federal Government to be the Katahdin Woods and Waters National Monument (monument) and, for the purpose of protecting those objects, reserve as a part thereof all lands and interests in lands owned or controlled by the Federal Government within the boundaries described on the accompanying map entitled, "Katahdin Woods and Waters National Monument," which is attached to and forms a part of this proclamation. The reserved Federal lands and interests in lands encompass approximately 87,500 acres. The boundaries described on the accompanying map are confined to the smallest area compatible with the proper care and management of the objects to be protected.

All Federal lands and interests in lands within the boundaries described on the accompanying map are hereby appropriated and withdrawn from all forms of entry, location, selection, sale, or other disposition under the public land laws, from location, entry, and patent under the mining laws, and from disposition under all laws relating to mineral and geothermal leasing.

The establishment of the monument is subject to valid existing rights, including the November 29, 2007, "Access Agreement" between EPI and the State of Maine, Department of Conservation that provides for certain public snowmobile use on specified parcels, and certain reservations of rights for Elliotsville Plantation, Inc., in specified parcels. If the Federal Government acquires any lands or interests in lands not owned or controlled by the Federal Government within the boundaries described on the accompanying map, such lands and interests in lands shall be reserved as a part of the monument, and objects identified above that are situated upon those lands and interests in lands shall be part of the monument, upon acquisition of ownership or control by the Federal Government.

The Secretary of the Interior (Secretary) shall manage these lands through the National Park Service, pursuant to applicable authorities and consistent with the valid existing rights and the purposes and provisions of this proclamation. As provided in the deeds, the Secretary shall allow hunting by the public on the parcels east of the East Branch of the Penobscot River in accordance with applicable law. The Secretary may restrict hunting in designated zones and during designated periods for reasons of public safety, administration, or resource protection. This proclamation will not otherwise affect the authority of the State of Maine with respect to hunting.

The Secretary shall prepare a management plan to implement the purposes of this proclamation, with full public involvement, within 3 years of the date of this proclamation. The Secretary shall use available authorities, as appropriate, to enter into agreements with others to address common interests and promote management needs and efficiencies.

Nothing in this proclamation shall be deemed to enlarge or diminish the rights of any Indian tribe. The Secretary shall, to the maximum extent permitted by law and in consultation with Indian tribes, ensure the protection of Indian sacred sites and cultural sites in the monument and provide access to the sites by members of Indian tribes for traditional cultural and customary uses, consistent with the American Indian Religious Freedom Act (42 U.S.C. 1996) and Executive Order 13007 of May 24, 1996 (Indian Sacred Sites).

Nothing in this proclamation shall be deemed to revoke any existing withdrawal, reservation, or appropriation; however, the monument shall be the dominant reservation.

Nothing in this proclamation shall preclude the use of existing low-level Military Training Routes, consistent with applicable Federal Aviation Administration regulations and guidance for overflights of military aircraft, consistent with the care and management of the objects to be protected.

Warning is hereby given to all unauthorized persons not to appropriate, injure, destroy, or remove any feature of this monument and not to locate or settle upon any of the lands thereof.

In Witness Whereof, I have hereunto set my hand this twenty-fourth day of August, in the year of our Lord two thousand sixteen, and of the Independence of the United States of America the two hundred and forty-first.

BARACK OBAMA

NOTES

Introduction

1. DeWolf, "East of Katahdin."
2. Ring, *Fifth Report of the Forest Commissioner*, 45–46.
3. The area of the purchase allowed the Penobscot River to reach the Canadian border.
4. Bennett, *Wilderness from Chamberland Farm*, 48.
5. Porter, *Bangor Historical Magazine*.
6. Currently called Medway.
7. Neff, personal communication re: Jonathan Maynard field notes, 1793.
8. After the dam was built, it became known as Grand Lake Matagamon.
9. Little, Neff and Whitcomb, *Penobscot East Branch Lands*.
10. Judd, Aroostook War and the Northeast Border.
11. Neff, *Katahdin*.
12. Hakola, *Legacy of a Lifetime*.
13. Raymond, personal communication re: 1839 road from Stacyville to the East Branch, 2018.
14. DeWolf, "East of Katahdin."
15. Avery, "Monument Line Surveyors," 33–44.
16. Judd, Aroostook War and the Northeast Border.
17. Raymond, "Mount Katahdin Road Company."
18. Raymond, personal communication re: 1839 road from Stacyville to the East Branch.
19. Dracup, "History of Geodetic Surveying."

20. Bureau of Parks and Lands, *Telos Dam and Cut (Canal)*.
21. Connolly, "What's Driving the Dispute."

Chapter 1

22. Smith, *Treasury of the Maine Woods*.
23. Geller, "Mount Katahdin—March 1853."
24. Neff, *Katahdin*.
25. Ibid.
26. Avery, "Story of the Wassataquoik, a Maine Epic," 83–96.
27. Geller, "Mount Katahdin—March 1853."
28. The 1849 four-part account can be found at Maine Memory Network, www.mainememory.net/artifact/18649.
29. Geller, "Mount Katahdin Peaks."
30. DeWolf, "East of Katahdin."
31. Huber, *Wildest Country*.
32. Lynch, *"Domestic Air" of Wilderness*.
33. Thoreau, *Maine Woods*.
34. Eckstorm, *Penobscot Man*.
35. Information about his trip came from Thoreau's last essay.
36. Emerson and Polis viewed wilderness and nature in much the same manner.
37. Lynch, *"Domestic Air" of Wilderness*.
38. Considered to be the father of conservation in our national parks.
39. Vietze, *Becoming Teddy Roosevelt*.
40. DeWolf, "East of Katahdin."
41. Staples, *Lewiston Journal Magazine*.
42. Conner, "O'er Katahdins Rugged Sides."
43. Hakola, *Legacy of a Lifetime*, 53.
44. Ibid., 70.
45. Whitcomb, *Governor Baxter's Magnificent Obsession*.
46. Holyoke, "Donn Fendler Remembered as 'True American Hero.'"

Chapter 2

47. Hakola, *Legacy of a Lifetime*.
48. Neff, *Katahdin*.

49. Raymond, personal communication re: 1839 road from Stacyville to the East Branch.
50. Avery, "Keep Path and Its Successors," 132–47.
51. Changes made in 1874 were due to the railroad.
52. Neff, *Katahdin*.
53. Personal communication with Ed Hendrickson of Brewer.
54. A ford is a shallow place with a solid bottom where the river may be crossed by wading or inside a wagon.
55. The cable ferry was operated from 1892 until 1922.
56. Avery, "Story of the Wassataquoik, a Maine Epic," 83–96.
57. A moraine is formed when the glacier stops retreating and deposits large numbers of extremely large boulders.
58. Find A Grave, "Marcus Rodman Keep."
59. Dean, "Maine Minutes," 57.
60. Avery, "Keep Path and Its Successors," 132–47.
61. Boone, "Wassataquoik History," 1–9.
62. See Neff, *Katahdin*, for an excellent history of the Wassataquoik.
63. Hakola, *Legacy of a Lifetime*.
64. Avery, "Keep Path and Its Successors (Concluded)," 224–37.
65. Hakola, *Legacy of a Lifetime*.
66. Staples, *Lewiston Journal Magazine*.
67. DeWolf, "East of Katahdin."
68. Avery, "Keep Path and Its Successors (Concluded)," 224–37.
69. Hooke and Hanson, "Late- and Post-Glacial History of the East Branch," 285–300.
70. Hakola, *Legacy of a Lifetime*.
71. Coolong, *History of Patten and Mount Chase*.
72. Shirley, "History Presented by American Thread."
73. Personal communication with Patten Lumbermen's Museum.
74. Johnston, "Matagamon."
75. Coolong, *History of Patten and Mount Chase*.
76. Williams, personal communication.
77. Mount Washington Auto Road, "History of the Road."
78. The Aroostook Road was built in 1840 to connect Molunkus to Fort Kent during the Aroostook War.
79. Avery, "Keep Path and Its Successors," 132–47.
80. Neff, *Katahdin*.
81. A chain was a standard unit of measurement. The chain contained one hundred links, each 7.92 inches, for a total of 66 feet.

82. Raymond, "Mount Katahdin Road Company."
83. Lord, "Ollie's Davidson."

Chapter 3

84. Personal communication with John W. Neff re: an intriguing Baxter-Hunt connection, 2017.
85. The Aroostook Trail had been spotted from Molunkus to T4 R6 in 1830 to bring settlers into the area.
86. Townships are primarily designated by the numbers 1 through 19 from south to north, while the ranges are counted from the easterly line toward the west. These numbers show the position in the state.
87. Coolong, *History of Patten and Mount Chase.*
88. Neff, personal communication re: Jonathan Maynard field notes, 1793.
89. Huntington, "Hunt Farm," 2–7.
90. Ibid.
91. GENi, "William H. Hunt."
92. Kimball, "Hunt's Farm," 12–15.
93. Huntington, "Hunt Farm," 2–7.
94. Chase, *History of Penobscot County, Maine.*
95. Neff, *Katahdin.*
96. Huntington, "Hunt Farm," 2–7.
97. Thoreau, *Maine Woods*, 34.
98. Little, Neff and Whitcomb, *Penobscot East Branch Lands.*
99. Avery, "Keep Path and Its Successors (Concluded)," 224–37.
100. Huntington, "Hunt Farm," 2–7.
101. Sambides, "Quimby Buys Historic Lunksoos Camps." The purchase amount was $334,539.
102. Austin, *Queen Bee.*

Chapter 4

103. Neff, *Katahdin.*
104. Bunting, *Day's Work.*
105. Neff, *Katahdin.*
106. Bunting, *Day's Work.*
107. Wood, "History of Lumbering in Maine."

108. Avery, "Keep Path and Its Successors," 132–47.
109. Bunting, *Day's Work*.
110. Avery, "Forest Fires at Mount Katahdin," 3, 4.
111. Neff, *Katahdin*.
112. DeWolf, "East of Katahdin."
113. Avery, "Keep Path and Its Successors," 132–47.
114. DeWolf, "East of Katahdin."
115. Avery, "Keep Path and Its Successors," 132–47.
116. DeWolf, "East of Katahdin."
117. Neff, *Katahdin*.

Chapter 5

118. Coolong, *History of Patten and Mount Chase*.
119. Garrett, *Life in a Logging Camp*.
120. Ibid.
121. Recollection Wisconsin, "Lumber Camp Life."
122. Nelligan, *White Pine Empire*.
123. Avery, "Story of the Wassataquoik, a Maine Epic," 83–96.

Chapter 6

124. McLeod, *The Northern*.
125. Burg, "Origins of the Lumberjack Breakfast."
126. Conclin, "Oh Boy, Did You Get Enough Pie?"
127. Ibid.
128. Ibid.
129. Kanes, *Cooks and Cookees*.
130. Holbrook, "Life of a 'Bull-Cook,'" 289–94.

Chapter 7

131. Goad, "Maine Used to Be the Ax-Making Capital of the World."
132. Peavey Manufacturing Company Catalogue, 2018.
133. Caulks, oddly enough, are pronounced "corks."
134. Ryan, "Straight to the Point."

135. Geller, *Within Katahdin's Realm.*
136. Bunting, *Day's Work.*
137. $5,000 in 1901 would be $150,000 today. Lombard made only eighty-three of the steam haulers between 1901 and 1917.
138. The term *freshet* is most commonly used to describe a spring thaw resulting from snowmelt and icemelt in rivers located in the northern latitudes of North America.
139. Bunting, *Day's Work.*
140. Kifner, "Last Log Drive in U.S. Floating to End in Maine."

Chapter 8

141. DeWolf, "East of Katahdin."
142. Smith, "Water Resources of the Penobscot River Basin Maine," 279.
143. U.S. Fish and Wildlife Service Northeast Region, "Charles Atkins."
144. Ibid.
145. DeWolf, "East of Katahdin."
146. Smith, "Reports of the Commissioner of Fisheries."
147. DeWolf, "East of Katahdin."
148. Smith, "Water Resources of the Penobscot River Basin Maine," 279.
149. Matthews, "Tenth Annual Report of the Bureau of Industrial and Labor Statistics."
150. Raymond, personal communication re: Bark Camp Meadow.
151. Lamey, *History of the Shoe Industry in Maine.*
152. Parsons, "Mt. Chase Fish-Feeding Station."

Chapter 9

153. MacEachern, "International Nature of the Miramichi Fire."
154. 5 million acres is equal to 7,400 square miles in total.
155. *New-York Weekly Tribune*, February 2, 1861.
156. Coolong, *History of Patten and Mount Chase.*
157. Avery, "Forest Fires at Mount Katahdin," 3, 4.
158. Boone, "Wassataquoik History," 1–9.
159. Ring, *Fifth Report of the Forest Commissioner.*
160. Boone, "Wassataquoik History," 1–9.
161. National Historic Lookout Register, "Deasey Mountain Lookout."

162. Noddin, "What Happened to Lieutenant Hare?"
163. Hilton, *Forest Fire Lookouts of Maine.*

Chapter 10

164. Johnson, "Alpine Glacial Features along the Chimney Pond Trail."
165. Rankin and Caldwell, *Guide to the Geology of Baxter Sate Park and Katahdin.*
166. Personal communication with Walter Anderson.
167. Neuman, "Bedrock Geology of the Shin Pond and Stacyville Quadrangles."
168. DeWolf, "East of Katahdin."
169. Hooke and Hanson, "Late- and Post-Glacial History of the East Branch," 285–300.
170. DeWolf, "East of Katahdin."
171. Neuman, "Bedrock Geology of the Shin Pond and Stacyville Quadrangles."
172. Doyle, "Owen Brook Limestone Prospect," 18–22.
173. Holmes, "Report of an Exploration and Survey."
174. Hitchcock, "General Report upon the Geology of Maine."
175. Berry, "Haskell Rock, East Branch Penobscot River."
176. Neuman, "Bedrock Geology of the Shin Pond and Stacyville Quadrangles."
177. Farnsworth, *Trout Brook Mountain.*
178. Ibid.
179. Caldwell, *Roadside Geology of Maine.*
180. Bennett, *Maine's Natural Heritage.*
181. Kelley and Dickson, "Maine's History of Sea-Level Changes."
182. Hall, Borns, Bromley and Lowell, "Age of the Pineo Ridge System," 344–56.
183. Hooke and Hanson, "Late- and Post-Glacial History of the East Branch," 285–300.
184. DeWolf, "East of Katahdin."
185. Ibid.

Chapter 11

186. DeWolf, "East of Katahdin."
187. Bennett, *Maine's Natural Heritage.*

188. Davis, *Bogs & Fens*.
189. DeWolf, "East of Katahdin."
190. Fafer and Schettig, *Ecological Characterization of the Maine Coast*.
191. DeWolf, "East of Katahdin."
192. Farnsworth, *Trout Brook Mountain*.
193. Soil composed of clay, silt, sand, gravel or similar detrital material deposited by running water.
194. Many of the maples have a DBH (diameter at breast height) of thirty-six inches or more.
195. Smith, "Water Resources of the Penobscot River Basin Maine," 279.
196. Ibid.
197. Rezneck, "Social History of an American Depression," 662–67.
198. Libby, "Freewill Baptist Church."
199. The report read: "Br. William M. Haskell, son of Mr. John and Mary Haskell of Poland, Me. Aged 25 years and 1 month, was drowned in Penobscot, E. Branch, June 19th, 1841 while breaking a jam on Grand Falls, which suddenly burst, affording no time to escape, either to shore or boat. Thus failing, he was swiftly carried down the stream about two hundred rods, and caught in one of the spine holes of a wing dam. The solemn tidings were soon conveyed home to the afflicted family. Elder George W. Haskell, his brother, immediately started for the fatal spot, and with the assistance of an Indian and one other man, succeeded in finding the body of his dear brother, after it had laid in the water twenty-two days. This was a matter of much satisfaction to him and his friends. But judge ye what must be his feelings, far from home in a wide wilderness, nineteen miles from any settlement, where with his hands he was subjected to the painful duty of assisting in preparing his coffin and grave, circumstances being such that he could not be moved. The last act being done, brother H. left the lonely and silent spot, and returned home in safety. We will now leave our brother in the grave, and call the attention of our readers to a more pleasing theme in relation to the life of the young man. Br. H. like many others, put off the subject of religion, or, in other words, did not give his heart to God, till a few months ago. During a protracted meeting last March in this place, he sought the lord and found him to the great joy of his heart. I think I never saw a more decided and happy convert. His prayers and exhortations will long be remembered in this region, and the prayer of the writer is that those young friends, whom he so affectionately entreated, may come and seek the lord. In this dispensation, aged parents are bereft of an affectionate son, and brothers and sisters of a dear brother."

Chapter 12

200. Hakola, *Legacy of a Lifetime*.
201. *Daily Kennebec Journal*, September 23, 1908.
202. Smith, "Water Resources of the Penobscot River Basin Maine," 279. When the Millinocket Mill opened, it was the world's largest paper mill, producing 240 tons per day of newsprint, 120 tons per day of sulfite pulp and 240 tons per day of ground wood pulp.
203. Hakola, *Legacy of a Lifetime*, 49.
204. Acadia National Park, "Acadia National Park History."
205. Hakola, *Legacy of a Lifetime*, 70.
206. Ibid.
207. Whitcomb, *Governor Baxter's Magnificent Obsession*.
208. Ibid.
209. This highlights some of the various trades, purchases and sales from the deeds made by Roxanne Quimby; there is a much more detailed account in the book *Queen Bee* by Phyllis Austin.
210. The parcels ranged in size from the 13.83-acre Lunksoos Parcel to the 12,063-acre Wassataquoik Parcel.

BIBLIOGRAPHY

Ahern, Jack. *Bound for Munsungun: The History of Early Sporting Camps in Northern Maine*. Bradford, MA: Pear Tree Publishing, 2008.

Austin, Phyllis. *Queen Bee: Roxanne Quimby, Burt's Bees, and Her Quest for a New National Park*. Thomaston, ME: Tilbury House, 2015.

———. "Quimby/Gardner Land Swap Will Protect Wassataquoik Stream and East of Baxter." *Maine Environmental News* (2015).

Avery, Myron. "Forest Fires at Mount Katahdin." *The Northern* (June 1928): 3, 4.

———. "Katahdin and Its History." *In the Maine Woods* (1935): 25.

———. "The Katahdinauguoh Explorations by an Enthusiast of Mountain-Climbing in Maine." *In the Maine Woods* (1929): 12–27.

———. "The Keep Path and Its Successors: The History of Katahdin from the East and North." *Appalachia* 17 (1928): 132–47.

———. "The Keep Path and Its Successors: The History of Katahdin from the East and North (Concluded)." *Appalachia* 17 (1929): 224–37.

———. "The Monument Line Surveyors on Katahdin." *Appalachia* 17 (1928): 33–44.

———. "The Story of the Wassataquoik, a Maine Epic." *Maine Naturalist* (September 1929): 83–96.

Bennett, D. *Wilderness from Chamberland Farm*. Washington, D.C.: Island Press, 2001.

Bennett, Dean B. *Maine's Natural Heritage: Rare Species and Unique Natural Features*. Camden, ME: Downeast Books, 1988.

Berry, Henry. "Haskell Rock, East Branch Penobscot River, T5 R8 WELS." Maine Geological Survey, October, 2005.

Boone, Gary. "A Wassataquoik History." *Forever Wild: Newsletter of the Friends of Baxter State Park* (Summer 2011): 1–9.

Bowley, Dianna. "Roxanne Quimby Discusses Her Plans for Her Wildlands." *Bangor Daily News*, May 6, 2011.

Bunting, William H. *A Day's Work: A Sampler of Historic Maine Photographs, 1860–1920*. Vols. 1 and 2. Thomaston, ME: Tilbury House Publishers, 1997.

Burg, Robert. "The Origins of the Lumberjack Breakfast." *Taste of the North Country*, June 26, 2014.

Caldwell, Dabney W. *Roadside Geology of Maine*. Missoula, MT: Mountain Press Publishing Company, 1988.

Chase, William. *History of Penobscot County, Maine*. Cleveland, OH: Williams, Chase & Company, 1882.

Conclin, Joseph. "Oh Boy, Did You Get Enough Pie?" *Journal of Forest History* (October 1979).

Conner, S.E. "O'er Katahdin's Rugged Sides." *In the Maine Woods* (1921).

Connolly, Alice. "What's Driving the Dispute Over U.S. Border Patrols and Canadian Fishermen Around Machias Seal Island?" *Global News*, July 5, 2018.

Coolong, Debbie. *The History of Patten and Mount Chase*. Mount Chase, ME: Oliver Press, 2017.

Cutter, William R. *New England Families Genealogical and Memorial*. New York. Lewis Historical Publishing Company, 1913.

Davis, Ronald. *Bogs & Fens*. Hanover, NH: University Press of New England, 2016.

Dawson, William F. "The Eastern Approach to Mt. Ktaadn." *Appalachia* 14 (1919): 353–56.

Dean, Robert W. "Maine Minutes." *General Conference and the Missionary Society* (1892): 57.

DeWolf, Bart. "East of Katahdin: Ecological Survey of the East Branch Properties of Elliotsville Plantation Inc., Penobscot County, 1914." Unpublished document.

Doyle, Robert G. "The Owen Brook Limestone Prospect, Penobscot County." *Contributions to the Geology of Maine*. Bulletin No. 18. Augusta: Maine Geological Survey, 1966.

Dracup, Joseph F. "History of Geodetic Surveying." *American Congress on Surveying and Mapping Bulletin* (March/April 1995).

Eckstorm, Fannie H. *The Penobscot Man*. Boston, MA: Houghton Mifflin Company, 1904.

Fafer, Stewart S., and Patricia A. Schettig. *An Ecological Characterization of the Maine Coast*. Newton, MA: Department of Interior Northeast Region, 1980.

Farnsworth, Roy L. *Trout Brook Mountain in Baxter State Park*. Millinocket, ME: Baxter State Park, 1994.

Garrett, Bob. *Life in a Logging Camp*. N.p., January 12, 2010. Archives of Michigan.

Geller, William. *Within Katahdin's Realm*. Farmington, ME: Mountain Explorations Publishing Company, 2018.

Geller, William W. "Mount Katahdin—March 1853: The Mysteries of an Ascent." Maine History Documents, Paper 119. 2016.

———. "The Mount Katahdin Peaks: The First 12 Women Climbers, 1849–1855." Maine History Documents, Paper 118. 2016.

Goad, Meredith. "Maine Used to Be the Ax-Making Capital of the World." *Portland Press Herald*, October 23, 2016.

Hakola, John W. *Legacy of a Lifetime: The Story of Baxter State Park*. Woolwich, ME: TBW Books, 1981.

Hale, Edward E. "An Early Ascent of Katahdin." *Appalachia* 9 (1901): 277–89.

Hall, Brad L., Hal W. Borns, G.R. Bromley and T.V. Lowell. "Age of the Pineo Ridge System: Implications for Behavior of the Laurentide Ice Sheet in Eastern Maine, U.S.A., during the Last Deglaciation." *Quaternary Science Reviews* 169 (August 2017): 344–56.

Hilton, David N. *Forest Fire Lookouts of Maine*. Greenville, ME: Moosehead Communications, 1997.

Hitchcock, Charles H. "General Report upon the Geology of Maine." In *Sixth Annual Report of the Secretary of the Maine Board of Agriculture*. Augusta, ME: Stevens & Seyward, Printers to the State, 1861.

———. "Geology of the Wild Lands." In *Sixth Annual Report of the Secretary of the Maine Board of Agriculture*. Augusta, ME: Stevens & Seyward, Printers to the State, 1861, 377–464.

Holbrook, Stewart. "The Life of a 'Bull-Cook': A Day in a 1920s Logging Camp." *Century Magazine* (July 1926): 289–94.

Holmes, E. "Report of an Exploration and Survey of the Territory on the Aroostook River during the Spring and Summer of 1838." Maine Board of Internal Improvements, August, Maine, 1839.

Holyoke, John. "Donn Fendler Remembered as 'True American Hero': Legend to Generations of Mainers." *Bangor Daily News*, October 11, 2016.

Hooke, Roger, and Paul Hanson. "Late- and Post-Glacial History of the East Branch of the Penobscot River, Maine, USA." *Atlantic Geology* 53 (2017): 285–300.

Huber, J. Parker. *The Wildest Country: A Guide to Thoreau's Maine*. Boston, MA: AMC Boston, 1981.

Huntington, Chris. "The Hunt Farm—A History." *Carl Sprinchorn News* 3 (1996): 2–7.

In the Maine Woods (1905): various pages.

Johnson, Robert A. "Alpine Glacial Features along the Chimney Pond Trail, Baxter State Park, Maine." Maine Geological Survey, September 2009.

Johnston, T. "Matagamon: A Short History." 1981. Unpublished document.

Judd, Richard. The Aroostook War and the Northeast Border. Maine Historical Society. https://www.mainememory.net/sitebuilder/site/781/page/1190/display.

Judd, Richard W., and E. Kellogg. *Ktaadn Trails: Lucius Merrill and the Paths to Katahdin*. Orono: University of Maine Publishing, 2005.

Kanes, Candace. "Cooks and Cookees: Lumber Camp Legends." Maine Memory Network, 2014. https://www.mainememory.net.

Kelley, Joseph T., and Stephen M. Dickson. "Maine's History of Sea-Level Changes." Maine Geological Survey, 1996.

Kifner, John. "Last Log Drive in U.S. Floating to End in Maine." *New York Times*, September 8, 1976.

Kimball, Marion R. "Hunt's Farm." *Down East* (April 1975): 12–15.

Lamey, M.H. *History of the Shoe Industry in Maine*. Boston, MA: Boston University, 1927.

Lewiston Evening Journal. "Daisey Dam, a Monument to a Drowned River Driver." Magazine Section, October 2, 1920.

Libby, James. "Freewill Baptist Church." *Poland News*, July 21, 1841.

Little, David, John Neff and Howard Whitcomb. *Penobscot East Branch Lands: A Journey through Time*. Portland, ME: Elliotsville Plantation, 2016.

Lord, Nina W. "Ollie's Davidson." 1987. Unpublished document.

Lynch, Thomas. *The "Domestic Air" of Wilderness: Henry Thoreau and Joe Polis in the Maine Woods*. Lincoln: University of Nebraska–Lincoln, October 1997. Faculty publication.

MacEachern, Alan. "The International Nature of the Miramichi Fire." *Forestry Chronicle* 90, no. 3 (2011): 334–37.

Matthews, Stephen W. "Tenth Annual Report of the Bureau of Industrial and Labor Statistics 1896." Augusta, Maine, 1896.

McLeod, John E. *The Northern—The Way I Remember*. Millinocket, ME: Great Northern Paper Company, 1982.

Neff, John W. *Katahdin: An Historic Journey*. Boston, MA: Appalachian Mountain Club Books, 2006.

———. Personal communication re: 1793 Jonathan Maynard field notes, 2017.

Nelligan, John E. *A White Pine Empire: The Life of a Lumbermen*. St. Cloud, MN: Northstar Press, 1969.

Neuman, Robert B. "Bedrock Geology of the Shin Pond and Stacyville Quadrangles, Penobscot County, Maine." U.S. Geological Survey, Professional Paper P0524-I. 1967.

Neuman, Robert B., and Douglas W. Rankin. "Bedrock Geology of the Shin Pond–Traveler Mountain Region." In *Guidebook to Field Trips in North-Central Maine*. Edited by L.S. Hanson and D.W. Caldwell. New England Intercollegiate Geological Conference, vol. 85. Augusta: Maine Geological Survey, 1995, 123–33.

Noddin, Peter. "What Happened to Lieutenant Hare?: A Maine Aviation Mystery." Millinocket, Maine—Katahdin Region, 2002. http: //www.katahdingateway.com.

The Northern 3. "Katahdin in Summer" (July 4, 1923).

———. "Sandy Stream and Mt. Katahdin" (May 2, 1923): 5.

Parsons, Will E. "The Mt. Chase Fish-Feeding Station." *In the Maine Woods* (1926).

Porter, Joseph W. *Bangor Historical Magazine*. Vol. 3. Bangor, ME: Benjamin Burr Print, 1888.

Rankin, Douglas W., and Dabney W. Caldwell. *A 2010 Guide to the Geology of Baxter Sate Park and Katahdin*. Maine Geological Survey, Department of Conservation.

Raymond, Earl. "The Mount Katahdin Road Company." *International Appalachian Trail News*, August 22, 2016.

———. Personal communication re: Bark Camp Meadow, 2018.

———. Personal communication re: 1839 road from Stacyville to the East Branch, 2018.

Rezneck, Samuel. "The Social History of an American Depression, 1837–1843." *American Historical Review* l, no. 4 (July 1935): 662–67.

Ring, E.E., Maine Forest Commissioner. *Fifth Report of the Forest Commissioner of the State of Maine*. Augusta, ME: Kennebec Journal Print, 1904.

Ryan, D. "Straight to the Point: What Are Those Spiked Boots?" *Washington Nature*, February 16, 2017.

Sambides, Nick. "Quimby Buys Historic Lunksoos Camps on Penobscot." *Bangor Daily News*, April 19, 2011.

Scribner's Monthly 16. "Camps and Tramps about Ktaadn" (May 1878): 33.

Shirley, B.A. "History Presented by American Thread." Milo Historical Society. Milo, Maine.

Smith, David. *A History of Lumbering in Maine, 1861–1960*. Orono: University of Maine Press, 1972.

Smith, Edmund W. *A Treasury of the Maine Woods*. New York: Frederick Fell Inc., 1958.

Smith, G.O. "Water Resources of the Penobscot River Basin Maine." Water Supply Paper 279. Washington, D.C.: United Sates Geological Survey, 1912.

Smith, Hugh M. "Reports of the Commissioner of Fisheries (Bureau of Fisheries) to the Secretary of Commerce and Labor for the Years ending June 30, 1903 through June 30, 1917." Washington, D.C.: U.S. Government Printing Office, 1917.

Staples, Arthur G. "Katahdin." *Lewiston Journal Magazine* (October 2, 1920).

Thompson, Woody B., and Hal Borns Jr. *Surficial Geologic Map of Maine*. Maine Geologic Survey, Department of Conservation, 1985.

Thoreau, Henry D. *The Maine Woods*. Boston, MA. Ticknor and Fields, 1864.

Vietze, Andrew. *Becoming Teddy Roosevelt: How a Maine Guide Inspired America's 26th President*. Rockport, ME: Down East Books, 2010.

Whitcomb, Howard R. *Governor Baxter's Magnificent Obsession: A Documentary History of Baxter State Park, 1931–2006*. Augusta, ME: J.S. McCarthy Printers, 2008.

Williams, Mike. Personal communication, 2018.

Wood, Richard G. "A History of Lumbering in Maine, 1820–1861." *Maine Studies*, no. 33 (1935).

Selected Webpages

Acadia National Park. "Acadia National Park History." https://acadiamagic.com.

Find A Grave. "Marcus Rodman." https://www.findagrave.com.

GENi. "William H. Hunt." https://www.geni.com/people/William-H-Hunt.

Maine Department of Agriculture, Conservation and Forestry—Bureau of Parks and Lands. "Telos Dam and Cut (Canal)." https://www.maine.gov/dacf.

Mount Washington Auto Road. "History of the Road." https://mtwashingtonautoroad.com.

National Historic Lookout Register. "Deasey Mountain Lookout." http://nhlr.org.

Recollection Wisconsin. "Lumber Camp Life." https://recollectionwisconsin.org.

State of Maine. "Bureau of Parks and Lands: Telos Dam and Cut." http://www.maine.gov.

U.S. Fish and Wildlife Service Northeast Region. "Charles Atkins: A Pioneer in Fisheries Conservation." https://usfwsnortheast.wordpress.com.

INDEX

W

ABOUT THE AUTHOR

Eric Hendrickson and his wife, Elaine, are both retired natural science educators currently living in Presque Isle, Maine. As a child, Eric lived in East Millinocket, being taught by his father from a very young age to have an appreciation for the outdoors and to understand the value of the cultural and natural history associated with the outdoors. As an adult, he has continued this love for exploring being awarded the Certificate of Merit for Exploration in 2002 by the National Speleological Society for contributions to the caving community. With the original purchases of the lands of the monument and the closing of it to hunting, it became an area for him to explore, with an emphasis on seeing both the natural and cultural history of the area with no particular focus. Traveling by mountain bike, as many of the roads were either closed to traffic or overgrown, he systematically explored the area, gaining a reputation for knowing where things could be located. When it was rumored that it might become a national park or monument, people in the area began to ask why they would make a park, as there was nothing special about the area. So, the focus of exploration changed to finding those things that made the area so special it would be worth to protecting for the people of America. After returning from a trip to Washington, D.C., to explain to the people at the Department of Interior what was so special about the area and what could be found there, the focus of exploration changed to finding and recording the old historical location to determine what might still be left at the sites. Once it became Katahdin Woods and Waters National Monument, Eric

The author giving a talk on the natural and cultural history of the Katahdin Woods and Waters National Monument at Orin Falls on the Wassataquoik Stream. *Michelle Benoit photograph.*

has acted as a leader for the monument and NPS staff regarding the history of those special locations. As the NPS regional archaeologist would say, he is continuing to work to learn to tell the story of the past by examining the land and the artifacts.